"Why, God? What are you doing, God? Qu
of faith and doubt can lead us to dea
Laurie's brilliant, biblical insights will h
God's mysterious perspective—a must read for following ,
especially when life's hard!"

John Burke, *New York Times* bestselling
author of *Imagine Heaven*

"As someone who struggled with their faith for years, I know
what it's like to doubt and question God. Laurie Short's writing
is covered in grace and patience, inspiring the reader to fall back
in love with their Creator. I wish I had this book years ago. The
trajectory of my life would have been quite different."

Zach Windahl, author of *The Bible Study*

"In the desperation that comes with the dark night of the soul, it
can be tempting to grab a biblical passage and hold on to it without fully understanding the context. The gift that Laurie gives
us with her study and insight is to help open us up to the unique
ways in which God may be speaking to us. Her lovely combina-
tion of heart and head speaks to all of us in ways that help us see
the light."

Nancy Ortberg, CEO, Tranforming the Bay with Christ

"Over the many years I have known Laurie Polich Short, she has
always been such an honest realist about faith and life. Her voice
here about faith and doubt rings with that same vigorous search-
ing, and practical help."

Mark Labberton, president, Fuller Theological Seminary

"As personal and cultural brokenness continue to overwhelm us,
thousands of self-help books are flying onto the shelves for our
supposed rescue. Maybe we need less self-help and more help
understanding where our help is coming from. This book could
not have come at a better time for our own personal walks, and
the real rescue that our culture and society are desperately search-
ing for."

Chris Brown, lead pastor, North Coast Church

"Does the Bible ever feel irrelevant? Do you wonder what God is
doing when your life feels like it is falling apart? If so, you will be
so encouraged by Laurie Short's new book. It will lead you to a

greater understanding of the ways God works and an assurance that He is trustworthy no matter what we face."

Becky Keife, author of *The Simple Difference* and *No Better Mom for the Job*

"Waiting is hard. Especially in our instant American culture. *Faith, Doubt, and God's Mysterious Timing* will provide you with an eternal perspective, remind you of the character of God, and enable you to embrace the mystery that is following Jesus in our broken world. I cannot endorse this book highly enough!"

Gary L. Gaddini, director, Unify

"If you yearn for more awareness of how Scripture speaks into our everyday realities, then let my dear friend Laurie Short listen with you. She hears God's voice in the text and invites all of us to trust that God is working even when we cannot see it."

Holly Beers, associate professor of religious studies, Westmont College; author of *A Week in the Life of a Greco-Roman Woman*

"Laurie Short has a way . . . a way of noticing, capturing, distilling, and telling the big story of faith that brings light into the room. When I hear her speak, I am drawn to the One she is describing. When I read her words, I find myself saying, 'Yes, that is it. God is like that!' She has a way of helping us faithfully hold the complexities of mystery."

Scott Lisea, campus pastor, Westmont Church

"Laurie Polich Short is one of the most authentic, insightful, and inspiring people I know. This book will bring you hope and wisdom. Laurie is an incredible communicator, and I found biblical help on every page. I highly recommend it."

Jim Burns, PhD, president, HomeWord; author of *Doing Life with Your Adult Children* and *Finding Joy in the Empty Nest*

"If you feel the challenge of connecting your faith journey with life's journey that leads you through the unpredictable or unexpected, then Laurie's words will serve as a guide to hope. Laurie has this amazing ability to help us find connection to and comfort in the One who holds the future in His hands and our hearts close to His."

Helen Musick, teacher, pastor, and author

Faith,
Doubt, and
**GOD'S
MYSTERIOUS
TIMING**

Faith, Doubt, and GOD'S MYSTERIOUS TIMING

30 BIBLICAL INSIGHTS ABOUT THE WAY GOD WORKS

Laurie Polich Short

BETHANY HOUSE
a division of Baker Publishing Group
Minneapolis, Minnesota

Published by Bethany House Publishers
Minneapolis, Minnesota
www.bethanyhouse.com

Bethany House Publishers is a division of
Baker Publishing Group, Grand Rapids, Michigan

Printed in the United States of America

Library of Congress Cataloging-in-Publication Data
Names: Polich-Short, Laurie, author.
Title: Faith, doubt, and God's mysterious timing : 30 biblical insights about the way
    God works / Laurie Polich Short.
Description: Minneapolis, Minnesota : Bethany House Publishers, a division of
    Baker Publishing Group, [2023]
Identifiers: LCCN 2022034462 | ISBN 9780764240027 (paperback) | ISBN
    9780764241598 (casebound) | ISBN 9781493440771 (ebook)
Subjects: LCSH: Providence and government of God—Christianity. | Faith. |
    Bible—Biography.
Classification: LCC BT135 .P65 2023 | DDC 231/.5—dc23/eng/20220830
LC record available at https://lccn.loc.gov/2022034462

Cover design by Rob Williams, InsideOut Creative Arts, Inc.

The author is represented by WordServe Literary Group, www.wordserveliterary.com.

Baker Publishing Group publications use paper produced from sustainable forestry practices and post-consumer waste whenever possible.

23 24 25 26 27 28 29   7 6 5 4 3 2 1

To those who walk in the dark,
who have no light,
trust in the name of the Lord
and rely on your God.

Contents

Introduction

Wonder what in the world God is doing?
You're in good company.

FAITH IS DEFINED as "confidence in what we hope for and assurance about what we do not see" (Hebrews 11:1). A paraphrase might be: *We can't see what God is doing, but we can absolutely trust what is happening outside our view.* No wonder our faith can wane. It's hard to hold on when our deepest prayer hangs in the air, seemingly unanswered. Or when circumstances we desperately wish would change instead drag on, with no end in sight.

Thankfully the Bible is full of people who experienced the same thing.

In their stories, we find our own stories. May some of the overlooked details in their stories bring encouragement to your soul. I started this exploration in my book *40 Verses to Ignite Your Faith* and found that many people were encouraged by verses they hadn't previously noticed. In this book, I will uncover more unnoticed verses in people's stories and make observations about the way God works that can help us hold on to our faith.

Because we have the advantage of reading these Bible stories years after they were lived, you will see how some stories continued to evolve after the people's lifetimes. But we will primarily look at how things evolved during their lifetimes—to help us suspend judgment on what is happening until more of the big picture becomes clear. Time can change the story.

For instance, Ruth accompanied her mother-in-law in her grief and ended up in Jesus's genealogy. Moses hid in the wilderness for forty years and, after he led thousands of Israelites through that same wilderness, saw the value of that seemingly lost time. Abigail risked her life to stop David from retaliating against her foolish husband, and after her husband died, David proposed and she married him. Servants obeyed a guest's request to fill jugs with water, and only after they poured wine out of those same jugs did they realize the power that guest held.

> The stories of Scripture show us that we often live our way into knowing, rather than know our way into living.

We have to live much of our lives by faith, not knowing exactly what God is doing. We may get a glimpse or a hint, but that is usually for the purpose of giving us confidence to live the unknown. The stories from Scripture show us that we often live our way into knowing, rather than know our way into living. Much of the timing and circumstances in our lives will be accurately interpreted only when we look back. What we are doing now may someday take on different meaning. In the meantime, there are insights from overlooked Scriptures that help us trust what we don't yet know.

The insights in this book will equip you to trust that God is alive and working even when you don't understand what is happening. If your faith grows to be confident in what you don't yet see, you will be more comfortable—and possibly even excited—to lean into the unknown. I am convinced that what God has in mind for your life is exponentially more than you can imagine. And there's a good chance that if God's timing seems wrong or too late, it will make your story outshine anything you could write.

1

More Is Happening
Than You Can See

A PAINTING FROM THE LATTER PART of the fifteenth century in the National Gallery in London bothered many who saw it, until a twentieth-century art critic looked more deeply into the story behind the painting.[1] And that caused everything to change.

The painting was called *The Virgin and Child with Saints Jerome and Dominic* by Filippino Lippi, and it had many of the elements of a masterpiece from the Renaissance era. But critics couldn't get past the obvious mistakes in the details. When scrutinized by even a slightly trained eye, the whole painting looked off—the direction of Mary's glance, the awkward position of the kneeling saints, and the hills in the background

1. Drew Williams, "Column: A New Perspective on Prayer," *Greenwich Sentinel*, January 17, 2017, https://www.greenwichsentinel.com/2017/01/17/column-a-new -perspective-on-prayer/.

that tumbled into the picture. While standing in front of the painting, art critic Robert Cumming was suddenly moved to research the story behind Lippi's work. He discovered that it had been commissioned for a prayer chapel and was meant to be viewed from a different angle than the gallery wall where it was displayed. Robert Cumming hurried back to the painting and dropped to his knees in front of it. When he did, the haphazardness disappeared. The story behind the painting gave him new eyes.

Our circumstances can be like this painting. The scene we are living appears disastrous, and we assume that what is in front of us is all that there is. If we look no further, what we see can lead us to incomplete conclusions. We might judge God's involvement or care based on what we see, but our perspective might change if we wait for more of the story to be revealed.

That's what happened to Robert Cumming when he probed the story behind Lippi's painting. Instead of living with his initial judgment, he took time to learn more, because he knew things about the artist that weren't compatible with the appearance of this particular work. Something urged him to look deeper into the artist's story, and when he did, he uncovered evidence that changed his view of the painting.

When scenes of our life look chaotic and troubling, we need to do the same with God.

Job shows us how.

JOB 42: A Broader View Clarifies Your Present View

What happens to Job is like the story of this painting—except the canvas is Job's life, and the apparent carelessness of the Artist has devastating consequences. Job feels completely abandoned by the God he has loved and served, and he has no idea why his circumstances have collapsed. His life shifts from immense success to abject tragedy in the first chapter of the book, and only we as readers know the backstory of the conversation between God and Satan. Job knows nothing of this backstory and spends most of the book crying out to the sky. However, in Job 42, Job does a complete turnaround. He moves from defiant rage to humble repentance, and he sees his circumstances in an entirely new light. He still knows nothing about the discussion between God and Satan and receives no particular answers about his suffering. What I want to explore is what turned Job's outrage into trust during this painful turn of his life.

Certainly it's not Job's friends or their advice; when they come to console Job, they tell him in several long-winded speeches that he must have done something really bad for this kind of suffering to happen to him. When they can't get Job to confess, they just keep talking—blasting him with their quid pro quo theology, which in Job's situation is neither accurate nor right. What is particularly sad is that Job is nursing a splintered heart and broken body while his friends pile reasons for his suffering on top of him (tips on how *not* to be a friend). What we know as readers is that the actual reason for Job's suffering is missing from what his friends present. Job suffered because Satan—not God—was blasting Job's life because of his faithfulness. The fact that God allowed Job's suffering was rooted in God's bet *against* Satan that Job's faith would endure. Job's friends were completely wrong—it was God's affirmation of Job, not God's punishment, that caused Job's painful circumstances to be reluctantly approved.

One of the many things the book of Job shows us is that we shouldn't make assumptions about God through what is happening in our circumstances. Our judgment of what is happening is incomplete until we allow time and understanding to reveal the truth of what we think we see. Job's friends judged

Job's situation based on what they saw, but just like the critics who initially judged Lippi's painting, they didn't have the full story. Job knew the truth of his innocence, and he persevered through tears and rage and unhelpful advice to get an audience with God. Finally, after thirty-five chapters of dialogue (mostly from Job's friends), just before the end of the book, God gives Job that chance.

Right before Job shouts "*Why?*" once more to the sky, a Voice thunders from the clouds to answer him. The Voice tells Job to brace himself, and it looks like Job is going to get his response.

> Our judgment of what is happening is incomplete until we allow time and understanding to reveal the truth of what we think we see.

"Where were you when I laid the earth's foundation?" the Voice asks, and Job is silent (Job 38:4).

"Who shut up the sea behind doors when it burst forth from the womb?" (v. 8).

In Job 38–41, God gives Job a world tour of creation, including all that is happening at any given moment around him. When Job gets a glimpse of the bigger story around his circumstances, it changes what he understands about his life. Job sits dumbfounded while God shows him all that is transpiring in the world at that moment. Job's questions about his suffering are silenced when God shouts new questions that Job never thought to ask. Here are some of them:

> "Who cuts a channel for the torrents of rain, and a path for the thunderstorm?" (Job 38:25).
>
> "Who has put wisdom in the inward parts or given understanding to the mind?" (Job 38:36 ESV).

"Who has the wisdom to count the clouds? Who can tip over the water jars of the heavens?" (Job 38:37).

"Who provides food for the raven when its young cry out to God?" (Job 38:41).

On and on God's questions thunder on top of Job, and he moves from wondering why he is suffering to how the world is spinning. While God shows him the details of creation, Job wakes up to all that happens while he breathes the air. Job gets a glimpse of the whole world—along with the immense power and exact timing it takes to run it. God never answers Job's questions about his suffering, but Job is overwhelmed by what he sees.

By looking at light, weather, stars, and nature, Job realizes that there is a broader view around his suffering that is enough to silence him. The bigger story exposes the limited view Job had of his life. This new, expansive view of God's creation gives Job the trust he needs to suspend judgment on his circumstances and hold on to his faith.

Job moves from rage to acceptance with these words:

I know that you can do all things; no purpose of yours can be thwarted. You asked, "Who is this that obscures my plans without knowledge?" Surely I spoke of things I did not understand, things too wonderful for me to know.

You said, "Listen now, and I will speak; I will question you, and you shall answer me." My ears had heard of you but now my eyes have seen you. Therefore I despise myself and repent in dust and ashes.

Job 42:2–6

Job is surprisingly subdued by the things God showed him. He never received an answer to his *why*, but four chapters filled with *who* took his need away. Like Robert Cumming, when Job found out more about the Artist's background story, it changed how he viewed his circumstances. The shift from *why* to *who* left him with the trust he needed to live his life.

In verse 3, Job uses the phrase "things too wonderful for me to know." You might expect him to say "things too *powerful*" or "things too *mighty*," but even when you go back to the original language of the text, Job is full of wonder in his response. Despite the suffering he's endured, Job appears to be awed, in a surprisingly good way, by God's goodness and majesty. The complexity of what was happening *around* his life gave him confidence to trust God *with* his life, even if he didn't understand all that was taking place. Waiting for more of the story can do the same for us.

Job shows us how to grow in our understanding of God when we don't understand what God is doing. When Job says, "My ears had heard of you but now my eyes have seen you" (Job 42:5), Job reveals that his faith is no longer secondhand. Job moves from hearing *about* God to hearing *from* God by pressing into his experience. Some of the answers his friends had given him didn't match what was happening to him, so Job sat with his questions and waited for God to speak.

Job's questions about his suffering weren't answered, but Job's response to God shows he was satisfied. Job's faith was restored—not by finding all the answers, but by what he was now able to see. Job was invited to look beyond his circumstances to what God was doing in the world around him. He could see how his life was part of a story so complex and detailed that his present circumstances might carry more (or different) meaning than he could now see. Time proved Job right.

It turned out to be Job's losses, not his blessings, that became the story that grew to define him. Job's cries and questions make up the biggest section of his story; it was his quest in suffering that God used most. Even though Job 42:12 declares, "The Lord blessed the latter part of Job's life more than the former part," we don't read that verse until the last chapter of his story. Forty-one chapters filled with heart-wrenching loss and agonizing questions are the bulk of the wisdom and meaning of Job's book.

The book of Job is supremely important to our faith because it reveals that God is not the author of suffering but our companion in it. We see this eventually through the life of Jesus, but here in the Old Testament, Job gives us a glimmer of that truth first. This important theology sets apart the book of Job with such significance that we can see a far-reaching purpose in Job's

> **God is not the author of suffering but our companion in it.**

suffering. Job couldn't see what his life would eventually mean to others, but his encounter with God moved him to trust. Job could see that the meaning of his story was beyond his scope.

The world Job was invited to see moved him to repentance for judging God on the limited view he had of his circumstances. What Job never saw until after his lifetime was the spiritual restoration that millions of suffering people have gotten from his gut-wrenching cries recorded in his book.

That is the mystery—and far-reaching effect—of the Artist's work.

GENESIS 50: Your Perspective Changes with Time

The story of Joseph is a sweeping saga that takes up thirteen chapters in Genesis. We don't often get that much of a person's story in Scripture, so it is worth looking at to trace God's hand through a lifelong journey of faith. When Joseph looks back, his reflections about what happened to him are filtered by what he now sees about his story. His words in Genesis 50:20 reveal that our perception of what happens to us may change as life unfolds. Looking back at Joseph's path, we see how things progress in ways we can't predict, and every leg of the journey has a purpose. The way our story gets put together is another indication that God is doing more than we can see.

Here's a snapshot of Joseph's story: when he is first introduced in Genesis 37, he is a teenager bragging about his dreams of greatness to his brothers. It turns out his dreams are a foreshadowing of what's to come, but announcing that his brothers will one day bow to him shows a lack of maturity for his future role. His brothers initially plot to kill him but then decide to sell him into slavery. Ironically, it is while Joseph is a slave that his gifts in leadership begin to shine.

> Never underestimate what God can do through circumstances you never would have guessed.

Never underestimate what God can do through circumstances you never would have guessed.

Joseph is eventually put in charge of his master's household, but the plot thickens when his master's wife tries to seduce him. Joseph admirably rejects her advances, but she cries rape, and Joseph is sent to jail. Two servants of Pharaoh's palace happen to be imprisoned at the same time as Joseph, and when both servants have dreams, Joseph uses his gift to interpret them. When one of the servants is released, he promises to remember Joseph when he gets out. Unfortunately, the servant forgets about Joseph until *two years* later, when Pharaoh has a dream that jostles the servant's memory. Joseph is brought out to interpret Pharaoh's dream, and when he accurately predicts a famine, he is released and immediately rises to power. The role Joseph plays during this worldwide famine causes him to have a different perspective when he looks back on all of his unfair circumstances.

Joseph is eventually reunited with his brothers because of his leadership in the famine, and he tells them to get their father and move to Egypt so Joseph can provide for all of them. The brothers are nervous that Joseph will punish them for what they did, so they bow before him, declaring they will be his slaves. In this moment, Joseph's adolescent dreams are realized; his response to them shows how differently he sees his circumstances now that he has seen more of life unfold:

> Don't be afraid. Am I in the place of God? You intended to harm me, but God intended it for good to accomplish what is now being done, the saving of many lives. So then, don't be afraid. I will provide for you and your children.
>
> Genesis 50:19–21

"You intended to harm me" is the rough truth of what happened. *"But God intended it for good"* is what God is able to do with the painful circumstances of our lives. God's work for our good doesn't minimize or take away the pain of our sufferings. Sometimes we read verses like this too fast—emphasizing God using our circumstances for good, while short-changing the pain that impacted our hearts. When Joseph saw his brothers' fear and remorse, he wept—partly from the sadness of what his brothers did to him. Loss is not absolved from our story even when we have a greater understanding of why that loss occurred.

The mystery that God takes our painful circumstances and works them into something good is a promise we see again and again in the Bible. However, God doesn't wipe all the pain away, partly because time can bring deeper healing than right after the pain occurred. Our future self will wrestle with our pain differently from our present self, because we'll have distance and perspective that we don't have while the painful circumstance is happening. God desires our healing and wholeness, and time is part of the canvas on which He works. When we reflect on our losses, often we realize we've become something we wouldn't be without them. Joseph's words in Genesis 50 show his growth in grace and humility, which God desires for us all. It's clear Joseph's losses have shaped his character and his heart.

When his brothers bowed down before him, Joseph could have responded by telling them they would pay for what they had done to him. But he saw all that had happened under the sovereignty of God.

When they first show up, Joseph's hurt is still fresh as he toys with his brothers (see Genesis 42–44). Eventually, he wails so loudly that the Egyptians in the next room hear him cry (Genesis 45). The toying and tears were part of Joseph's process of getting to forgiveness for all that had happened to him. We get to read all of this in Joseph's story, and it helps us see how living by faith is more complicated than applying a promise from a verse. That's the benefit of getting to read the details of the long, full story of his life.

When Joseph weeps in Genesis 50:17, it is apparent that his brothers' message still triggers him. Even though Joseph has a broader perspective of what happened to him, it strikes a nerve in his heart. But unlike the adolescent who told his brothers that they would one day bow to him, Joseph now places himself *with* them *under* God's sovereignty in how he responds to them. He sees his position of leadership as something God gave him— and believes God lined up all the circumstances that brought him to this place. Joseph is also able to see that his brothers' actions—terrible as they were—sparked the series of events that brought him to Egypt. Seeing God's hand in the macro story shifts Joseph's perspective of the micro story, which allows him to treat his brothers with grace. It can do the same for us.

In some ways, Joseph came to the same place as Job; when he saw God's grand design, it changed how he viewed his story. For Job, it happened because he saw all that God was doing in the world; for Joseph, it was because he saw all that God did by looking back over his life. In Job's story, the largeness of the world—with all the complexity of how things fit together—gave Job new understanding. For Joseph, the big story of saving many lives reinterpreted the small story of unfair circumstances that he had endured. Both men still had pain, but they saw a bigger picture around their pain that helped them face it with trust.

In both stories there was loss and hardship, along with favor and blessing. God shaped each of these men through their hardships, and they *still carried pain* when the blessings came. Pain is the teacher we don't want, yet often need, for the character God wants to build within us. No life escapes pain, so God must have a purpose for allowing it to shape who we become. C. S. Lewis says, "God whispers to us in our pleasures . . . but shouts in our pain,"[2] and I would add that we sometimes *need* pain's interruption to recognize God's goodness. Everything we have is a gift, but our gifts evolve into expectations until pain awakens the awareness that they could be lost.

Pain shaped both Job and Joseph; not only did they see their stories differently, *they* became different. Job moved from rage to repentance; Joseph looked back on his life and saw God's mercy in every good and bad part. Through Joseph and Job, we learn that the end of our story may give new meaning to the beginning. This encourages us to hold on and wait, especially during dark chapters in our journey of faith.

2. C. S. Lewis, *The Problem of Pain* (New York: Macmillan, 1956), 81.

If we know that the end of the story will bring new meaning to the beginning, it can help us suspend judgment on our current circumstances. We typically judge what *will* happen based on what *is* happening, and that's not necessarily what unfolds. Joseph's story shows us that where a prison sentence normally leads could be miles away from what actually happens. Job's story reveals that the one who doesn't have the answers about why bad things happened to him could be the person God uses to instruct people who think they do.

> **We typically judge what *will* happen based on what *is* happening, and that's not necessarily what unfolds.**

God is capable of bringing good from bad, life from what's lifeless, and meaning from our sorrow—and at any moment He can do the same in your circumstances. We can live the hardship of our moments without letting them write the script for the rest of our life. Observing the unpredictable way God works helps us look at our story with new hope.

MATTHEW 1: God Is Seen in the Details

Joseph and Job reveal that sometimes we need to look at the bigger picture around our circumstances to see how God is working. But we can also find evidence of God by doing the opposite—we can look closely at the details of our lives that expose God's touch. In the big and the small, we can observe that God is at work doing more than we can see.

The genealogy in Matthew 1 is one place to notice God's detail by looking at the chain of people woven into Jesus's backstory. One verse where we find a special showcase of God's work is in the connection between two of the women who are listed in Jesus's family line. Like the rest of the genealogy, Matthew 1:5 gives a statement that we might overlook in the boredom of reading genealogies. But if we stop and look deeper into the relationships included in this verse, we can see God's orchestration in the story behind the details. Noticing these details can strengthen our faith.

Matthew 1:5 reads, "Salmon the father of Boaz, whose mother was Rahab, Boaz the father of Obed, whose mother was Ruth."

The verse continues, but let's pause here and look deeper into these relationships. Rahab is the prostitute from Jericho introduced in Joshua 2, and she is mentioned again in Joshua 6. She is the one who hides Joshua and the Israelite spies on the roof of her brothel while they scope out their battle plan, and she ends up going with them after her city is destroyed. Every time Rahab is referenced in the Bible, she is called "Rahab the prostitute" (or harlot), an unfortunate label she continued to carry even into the New Testament. Here in Matthew 1, however, there is no label of prostitute included behind her name. Rahab is listed in this verse not as a prostitute but as a wife and a mother. She has the honor of being one of only five women listed in the chapter that traces the lineage from Abraham to Jesus.

Rahab is mentioned later in Hebrews 11 and James 2 because of her great faith in taking a risk to side with the Israelites. But Matthew 1:5 is the only place in Scripture that shows that Rahab was more than a prostitute; she became part of the line of Jesus because she was Salmon's wife. Verse 5 also reveals that Rahab had a son named Boaz, and if you've read the book of Ruth, that name might be familiar to you. Boaz is the wealthy landowner who generously provides grain for Ruth and Naomi, and he eventually marries Ruth. This verse in Matthew 1 not only shows how God blessed Rahab's life by bringing her a husband and a son, it infers that Ruth and Rahab are brought together as family. Though Scripture is silent about this storyline except in this verse, when Ruth marries Boaz, Rahab becomes the mother-in-law of Ruth. And if you know anything about Ruth's story, you know that Rahab is not the first to occupy that role.

Ruth was a Moabite who became part of the Jewish community because she made a commitment to stay with her first mother-in-law, Naomi, after tragedy struck. Naomi ended up bringing Ruth into the Jewish faith and culture and changing Ruth's life. What only God saw at this crossroads was how Ruth and Rahab would ultimately be connected in their stories. Through Ruth's journey in following her first mother-in-law, she ended up acquiring Rahab as a second mother-in-law, and both Ruth and Rahab are included in Jesus's line.

Naomi is the unwritten part of Matthew 1:5, but she is the reason for the relationship between Ruth and Boaz. So this line in the genealogy illustrates the connection and redemption of three lives—a former prostitute and two widows—all included in the backstory of this verse. Unless we take time to observe these details, like many details in our lives, they could easily be missed.

Matthew 1:5 offers us a microscope to see how God is at work in the details. So much of God's work is there for us to notice or miss—and certainly that is true in the brevity of this verse. There are so many backstories packed into Jesus's genealogy, and this gives us the scope of the canvas on which God is working. We may not be able to see all that is happening in the relationships and connections around us, but when we notice the way things evolve over time, we have a more complete picture of the way God works. Things that feel jumbled and disjointed right now may have more meaning through connections we see when we look back.

This may be a good place for you to pause over your own story and remember something in your past that has evolved over time to take on new meaning. When I got engaged to—and didn't end up marrying—a man who had two children, my grief turned to gratitude years later when I met my husband. But at the time, there was great confusion—not only in my heartbreak with my fiancé but in the loss of my sweet relationship with his eight-year-old little girl. Years later, however, when I married a man with a six-year-old boy who became my stepson, I looked back on that relationship with my fiancé's daughter and saw new purpose in it that I couldn't see earlier. That relationship suddenly took on new meaning, because it prepared me for the boy who would eventually take her place.

Many details of our lives go unnoticed because we don't take time to recognize or acknowledge them. We may overlook them as coincidences or haphazard details, but this keeps us from noticing the fingerprints of God. We could skim Matthew 1:5 in the genealogy of Jesus and miss the details of the intertwined stories. In the same way, I could remember my relationship with my former fiancé as an arbitrary disaster and never make any connection with how it prepared me for my future stepparenting role. The evidence of God's touch whispers rather than shouts, leaving us to tune in to recognize it. But when we do, it strengthens our resolve to trust Him in the midst of things that we don't understand, and wait things out.

Certainly we see that looking back at Joseph; so many details in his life were reinterpreted at the end of his story. God used every leg of his journey, but while he was living it, the timing and difficulty of his circumstances made God's plan impossible to see. Taking the time to look back over our lives helps us see more of God's orchestration in the confusing things that happen. When we see how God has used our pain and difficulty, we can persevere through the suffering and uncertainty we might be experiencing now.

The presence of God is invisible, but there are stories in the Bible that help us learn what to look for to witness it. The rest of this book will explore more of these stories to help you notice some ways that God works that you might not have seen. My hope is that these insights will encourage you to press on in the parts of your story that seem to reflect God's indifference or absence. Waiting for what unfolds might reinterpret what you see.

As Robert Cumming discovered, something may be off in the picture in front of you because you don't yet know why it belongs.

REFLECTION QUESTIONS

1. In Job 42:1–6, Job reflected on his new understanding that his life was part of a bigger story and that his circumstances might carry a different meaning than he could presently see. How does that speak to your own life? Is there something you are going through where this perspective might help?

2. Looking at what Joseph learned at the end of his story in Genesis 50, has your perspective of something difficult that God allowed in your life ever changed with time? If so, how did it change?

3. When you look at Matthew 1:5 and how God orchestrated the details of these women's stories, what insight does it give you into how God might be working in your life? Can you see God in any details that you may have overlooked?

2

Time Is Never Lost

TIME IS A MOVING TARGET. It is measured differently depending on what fills its space. It drags on endlessly through loss and hardship. It leaps without warning when a child leaves home. And when someone you love dies, you have a sudden awareness that a chunk of it passed before you could blink.

When it comes to our spiritual lives, our timing and God's timing are almost always different. Things happen too soon—or too late—and we feel forgotten or unprepared. When it comes to our prayers, time can drag on until we may question God's existence. Especially when we read Bible stories where giant seas part, babies are born to geriatric couples, and God delivers food from the sky. It's no wonder our faith grows dull when we experience God's silence for a year.

What we tend to overlook is that the giant seas parted after *four hundred years* of slavery. A baby was born to an elderly couple *ten years* after the already late promise. Food was delivered from the sky, but it turned to maggots if anyone tried to save it until morning. The timing involved in these Bible stories reveals that the people living them then needed as much faith as our current stories need now. One thing is clear: timing is often what God uses to grow our faith.

When things aren't happening when we want them to happen, we feel time has been lost. But time itself is never lost; we only lose what we may have wanted that time to be. Because I didn't marry until I was forty-nine, I know by experience that waiting for what you want can make you feel forgotten. Looking back, I see how God used my time of singleness for some things that happened that were bigger than I prayed. I begged God for marriage, then went through two devastating breakups and a broken engagement, which healed my heart in ways I didn't know needed healing. I cried out to be a mom, and God brought me a pregnant teen in my youth group, followed by an inner-city girl who needed my help. The fifteen years of unwanted singleness were filled with nothing that I asked for, but they were also filled with a richness of learning that healed me, used me, and prepared me for what was coming. The time during which I felt like I was wallowing in God's indifference was used to bring some indispensable glimpses of Him into my life.

God also used that time to help me let go of things I wanted so I could be open to the things God had for me. God's waits always have a purpose, and we usually only see that purpose fully when we look back. Unwanted detours lead to experiences and relationships that eventually become indispensable to our stories. In the passages that follow, you'll see that is as true for people in the Bible as it is for us. Whether the wait is used to line things up, work in our hearts, or prepare us for a miracle, the purpose of our waits can be seen more clearly when we see what happens next in our life.

Perhaps the most important truth about God's waits is that they pry open our hands from the things we are clinging to for our future. Then we can be open to the One who has a bigger plan—and see, by what unfolds, how He's been clinging to us.

EXODUS 2: Waits Are for a Purpose

The story of Moses is divided into three parts, and the part we know least about is the forty years in the middle of his story. The Bible gives us only a few lines to mine of this in-between time. This part of Moses's story is the period between when he runs away from Egypt and when he returns to rescue the Israelites. This middle part of his story is documented in the last half of Exodus 2, but very little is said about what happened during this chapter of Moses's life. However, if we take a closer look, we can see how God used this seemingly nondescript season in Midian to equip Moses for what was ahead.

There is one incidental phrase in Exodus 2:23, and a subsequent reference in Acts 7, that tells what happened during the time Moses was in Midian. In Acts 7:30, Stephen mentions in his speech that the period lasted forty years, but in Exodus 2 we are not given the specific amount of time. What we do discover is what was happening with the Israelites in Egypt after Moses ran away to Midian. We are given some idea of the increased suffering of those he left behind here:

> During that long period, the king of Egypt died. The Israelites groaned in their slavery and cried out, and their cry for help because of their slavery went up to God.
>
> Exodus 2:23

We have very few clues about what that time in the Midian wilderness was like for Moses. The only hint we have of his feelings during that season is that Moses names his son Gershom—which unfortunately for Gershom means "alien" or "foreigner"—and then proclaims, "I have become a foreigner in a foreign land" (Exodus 2:22). We can assume Moses probably thought this foreign-land chapter of his life would last the rest of his days, but we know from looking back that this season was only a preparation for the next chapter of his story. However, Moses didn't know that while living it, and that's the first insight we can glean from this unobtrusive part of his life.

While Moses thought he would probably be tending sheep in the wilderness for the rest of his life, God was giving him the experience he needed for shepherding thousands of Israelites. There would be many weeks and months that he would be leading people through the wilderness in the future, so God gave him this time as his practice run. If Moses had gone straight from a privileged childhood in Egypt to his encounter at the burning bush, he wouldn't have been equipped for what lay ahead for him. This observation can help us look at our own in-between seasons differently—especially when it seems there is no point or any change in sight. What happens to Moses after this period urges us to suspend judgment on what things look like now—and trust God for what our waiting period could become.

It was in Exodus 2 that Moses went from being raised in an Egyptian palace to being part of a humble Midianite priest's family. Through the generosity of Jethro the priest (also called Reuel), Moses was not only gifted with marriage to his daughter Zipporah (see Exodus 2:21–22) but presumably given the job of tending Jethro's flocks. Scripture is silent about Moses's occupation until we read about him tending Jethro's sheep in Exodus 3:1, but we can assume he spent most of his time shepherding. The important insight here is that Moses had no idea it was preparation for his adventure to come. One day he would exchange sheep for people, and having a knowledge of wilderness living would be indispensable for what God would call Moses to do.

We also see in Exodus 2:23 that this in-between time was instrumental in ushering in a new Pharaoh in Egypt, which set up the drama that was coming. This new Pharaoh would likely have more of a brotherly knowledge of Moses than a fatherly one, since they were presumably raised together when they were boys. The details of their relationship aren't included, but we know from Exodus 2:10 that the previous Pharaoh's daughter raised Moses. So, we can assume that Moses was acquainted with the new Pharaoh; however, we are left to speculate (or watch *The Prince of Egypt*) to imagine what their relationship had been. We only know what happened in their relationship years later, when God sent Moses to confront him, and they were both many years older. If there had been any childhood friendship, by the time Moses saw Pharaoh again, the warmth that might have once been between them clearly had passed.

Exodus 2:23 says that during Moses's stay in Midian, not only was another king put in place, but the Israelites groaned under increasing hardship. Their slavery made them miserable, and they undoubtedly longed for the rescue that they didn't know God was setting up. Unbeknownst to Moses while he quietly tended sheep, God was going to pull him from obscurity to be the leader of the most acclaimed rescue in the Old Testament. Moses was eighty years old when God used him to rescue the Israelites, and this chapter reveals that we have no idea during our waits what God may be lining up.

Another faith-inspiring detail from this part of Moses's life is the relationship that developed between Jethro and Moses during his time in Midian. Because Moses had been raised in an Egyptian palace without his biological mother or father, it's poignant that God brought Moses a father-in-law who immediately took him into his family and into his life. Jethro didn't only give Moses his daughter Zipporah; other passages show he became a father figure for Moses. In Exodus 4:18, Jethro blesses Moses before he returns to Egypt. In Exodus 18, Jethro visits Moses in one of the most famous scenes of Moses's life. Jethro observes Moses after he's rescued the Israelites and as he is trying to make decisions for hordes of people under his leadership. Jethro speaks tenderly to his son-in-law and advises Moses to delegate his authority, because he sees Moses is in over his head. Out of concern for Moses's health, Jethro prompts Moses to choose capable leaders to assist him in governing the people (see Exodus 18:26). Moses's respect for Jethro is evident in Exodus 18:24: "Moses listened to his father-in-law and did everything he said."

These observations help us to see that the in-between season of Moses's life turned out to be one of the most important chapters in his story. Without this time, Moses would have been ill-prepared for the incredible chapter God was about to bring into his life. It was in the middle of this mundane period of tending sheep that Moses was in the right place to observe a bush that was burning. God used the time in the wilderness not only to cultivate Moses's leadership but to position him for a conversation at the bush that would change his life. In front of that bush, Moses's wandering came to an end, and he was called to the most renowned chapter of his life.

GENESIS 17: Our Clocks Make Room for Miracles

Long waits shrink our faith with a slow burn of disappointment. We might begin them with the belief that God can do anything, but the length of our wait can slowly beat the hope out of our heart. In Genesis 17, the Bible figure most renowned for his faith is definitely in that place.

Abraham has already been met by God twice, and the second time he was told a child was coming. He was old and childless with a barren wife, yet as a tribute to his great faith, he immediately believed what God said. Genesis 15:6 proclaims, "Abram believed the Lord," and this is the first time that faith is credited as righteousness in God's sight.

Fast-forward to Genesis 17; God meets Abraham again, and many years have passed without the promised child. During the in-between time, Abraham fathered a child with Sarah's maidservant Hagar (at Sarah's suggestion), and since Abraham was eighty-six when that son was born, he surmised that Ishmael would be the only child he would have. However, in Genesis 17:16, God tells him another child is still coming. If you've ever given up waiting for something you desperately wanted, you'll be able to relate to Abraham's response:

> Abraham fell facedown; he laughed and said to himself, "Will a son be born to a man a hundred years old? Will Sarah bear a child at the age of ninety?"
>
> Genesis 17:17

Gone is the confidence Abraham had in Genesis 15:6, when he responded by believing. Abraham's question about Sarah seems almost to be added for emphasis, to accentuate the ridiculousness of bearing a child at that age. Like us, Abraham can't believe what time has made impossible. He begs God for Ishmael to receive God's blessing because it seems clear that Ishmael is the only son he will have (Genesis 17:18). This is a different response from what Abraham proclaimed in chapter 15, when God first announced to him that he would have a child. Abraham's request that Ishmael could live under God's blessing shows that time has beat down his belief.

God not only assures Abraham that a second son will still come, but it is apparent that He was waiting for the clock to run out before delivering the miracle. Isaac's name will be a tribute to Abraham's wait; because Isaac means "laughter," he would forever be a symbol of Abraham and Sarah's incredulous joy. God doesn't condemn Abraham for laughing in this chapter. Instead, God joins Abraham in the midst of his inability to believe and adds an exclamation point by telling him to name the child "Laughter" to remember his response. This passage testifies that God delights in blowing us away, and when we have to wait until circumstances seem impossible, our faith is forever changed when God shows up.

It is our greatest doubts that surprisingly form the route to a greater faith.

This passage also gives us the comforting insight that God is not dependent on our response to perform a miracle. We might even go so far as to say that God understands when our faith has waned because of the disappointment we've had to survive. Abraham started his journey in confidence when he was in his eighties. After years passed, Sarah presented him with the idea to father a child through Hagar, which he accepted, and then believed this would be the only child he would have. Genesis 17:1 says *thirteen years later*, when Abraham is *ninety-nine* years old, God tells him he and Sarah are still going to have a child. His laughter reveals how his faith has been beaten down by the waiting; he has accepted the circumstances he has rather than holding on to a future for which he once hoped. Abraham thinks it is too late for that future, but he is about to learn that "too late" is the timing God waits for to shine.

> "Too late" is the timing God waits for to shine.

When things happen when they are *supposed* to happen, we celebrate. When things happen when they are *not* supposed to happen, we worship—because that's when God's power is clearly displayed. God wanted Abraham's descendants to originate from a God-breathed biological miracle. We might pause here to contemplate whether Isaac's birth is a fore-shadowing of the even bigger miracle God would bring forth from a virgin's womb. Whatever God's intention is with birthing Isaac this late in Abraham's life, we see in this passage that God doesn't do this miracle *because* of Abraham's faith—God does this miracle to provoke Abraham's faith. God already knew Abraham was a man of great faith, but it is possible God wanted to stretch him *past his ability to believe* so his faith would grow. We often think that God's miracles happen because of our belief, but this passage indicates that sometimes they happen in spite of it. God isn't dependent on the size of our faith for what his power can achieve.

God certainly desires faith, and this is clear in Genesis 15:6, when Abraham's faith is counted by God as righteousness. But this passage in Genesis 17 reveals the amazing insight that God understands the strain on faith that can happen, especially when time takes its toll on our hearts. Sometimes we live so long with an unmet desire that we learn to accept our undesired circumstances. *What if* gets drowned by the longevity of *What is*, and our hearts don't have the energy to imagine that things could still change. This passage confirms that God joins us at the place where our faith ends and leads us to where a new and stronger faith begins.

In Genesis 18 we see how God meets Sarah too, and it happens in the form of three mysterious visitors. Abraham goes outside to offer the visitors something to eat, and Sarah overhears the news that she will have a baby—news her husband has already heard. It is possible that Abraham didn't tell Sarah about his previous encounter with God because he wanted to protect her from further disappointment. When Sarah hears the visitors' news, she, like Abraham, laughs out loud before she can subdue her disbelief (see Genesis 18:12). When the visitors hear and confront her, she is too afraid to admit she was laughing. She later discovers in Genesis 21 that *Laughter* is the name her son would come to be called.

Sarah muses to herself, "After I am worn out and my lord is old, will I now have this pleasure?" (Genesis 18:12).

Our doubts are stirred by Sarah's question: can something we've longed for, and finally accepted as no longer possible, still be God's plan for us? Abraham and Sarah's story proclaims a resounding *yes*—and it is an encouragement that things that have passed us by may still be in the cards. Because I married late in life, people who still long for marriage say to me, "You give me hope that it can still happen." Perhaps that's part of why God allows our waits, so our story can be a testimony for others who need our story to persevere in their own. When God gives us something after it's too late, it gives people hope that a prayer they've let time extinguish could still happen. If we can let go of the timeline we wanted, it gives God room to choose the time it comes—and this increases the celebration when it arrives.

The later it comes, the more of a miracle it will be.

ACTS 16 and PHILIPPIANS 1: Things Line Up beyond Our Scope

Time is viewed differently in retrospect. We get a glimpse of things that weren't in our view at the time they were lived. Looking back, we see that detours we never would have chosen became some of the most precious parts of our stories. People we never would have met, because of circumstances we didn't ask for, have changed who we've become. We might even see how the routes we *didn't* choose had the greatest impact on our lives because of what God did with our unwanted circumstances. Certainly that was true of the apostle Paul.

Acts 16 reveals that because Paul was derailed in his original plans, he ended up meeting the people who became the church of Philippi. They were the original recipients of Paul's stirring words in the book of Philippians, which has been used by God to transform millions of lives. Paul didn't know that his letter to the Philippians (along with his other prison letters) would eventually form much of the New Testament and reach multiple generations. However, what he did know—partly based on his experience in Philippi—was that wherever he was sent, God had a plan for each chapter of his life. That may be part of the reason that in Philippians 1:12, Paul proclaims these prophetic words about being in prison: "I want to you know, brothers and sisters, that what has happened to me has actually served to advance the gospel."

> God uses unplanned diversions that may appear to be wasted time to line things up beyond our scope.

It's clear Paul trusted that his imprisonment was part of God's orchestration. What he couldn't see was how, after his lifetime, his prison letters would end up becoming the farthest-reaching ministry of his life.

Looking deeper into the story of the Philippian church, Paul's experiences had already reinforced his belief that God's purposes were beyond our understanding. Paul learned to submit to God's leading, so he knew that wherever he was sent, it would somehow be used to advance the kingdom of God. Yet he didn't know the extent of the reach he would have while he was *in* prison. What is also striking is that the letter to the Philippians was written for people Paul never would have met if God hadn't interrupted his route. The way the church in Philippi came to be is another example of how God uses unplanned diversions that may appear to be wasted time to line things up beyond our scope.

Acts 16 gives us the Philippian backstory—it reveals that Paul planned to go to Bithynia, but he was blocked in his intended route by the Spirit of Jesus (v. 7). Paul has a vision of a man from Macedonia (where the city of Philippi was located), who begs Paul and his companions to come (vv. 7–8). Concluding that this change of direction was from God, Paul and his companions set sail for Macedonia and arrive at Philippi. This interruption gave the church of Philippians its start.

What you picture when you hear "the Philippian church" is probably not the same as the cadre of believers in Philippi who responded to Paul's message. The people were quite a diverse group, and it was actually in the home of a woman named Lydia where this band of believers started to meet. When Paul first arrived in Philippi, he expected to find a place of prayer by the city gates. When he didn't see one, he started speaking to some women who were gathered there, and they were the first audience Paul shared the gospel with after he arrived. A woman named Lydia was among them—and she is the only one named of the group who responded to Paul's message. She is referred to as "a dealer in purple cloth" and "a worshiper of God" (Acts 16:14), which indicates not only that she had money and influence but that she had a reverence for God even before Paul arrived.

When Lydia heard Paul speak, "The Lord opened her heart to respond to Paul's message" (Acts 16:14). Since she is the only Philippian believer named in the entire chapter, it can be assumed she had some influence on how the Philippian church began. It is unclear whether Lydia was married, single, or widowed, but verse 15 refers to others as "members of her household," which indicates that she was the leader of her home. Roman culture referred to women mostly in relationship to their husbands, so the way Lydia is described is unusual, and could mean that she was possibly living alone with children or extended family. Paul seems to have considered her to be a strategic partner in the Philippian church, because he mentions her home as a place of meeting twice. She invites Paul and his companions to come to her home in verse 15, and her house is mentioned again in verse 40 as the place where an increasing number of believers continued to meet. Lydia's home was likely the place where the church of Philippi had its start.

The group of believers that begins with Lydia and her household grows to include a jailer and his family after an earthquake shakes the prison walls where Paul and Silas were held captive (Acts 16:34). Paul and Silas's response of staying in prison so the jailer wouldn't get in trouble becomes the turning point for the jailer to come to faith (Acts 16:29–31). So God uses a redirected journey, a wealthy woman who opens her home, and an earthquake in a jail cell to form the church of the Philippians in a way that was unimaginable. It's an illustration of how God weaves things together in such a way that what is actually happening can't be seen until you look back. While you are living your life, you can't imagine how God will weave together the haphazard circumstances included in your route.

However strangely this small group of believers began, they grew into one of Paul's most precious churches, full of sacrificial people. It's clear from Paul's writing that this little church grew to occupy a prominent place in his heart. His words to them in Philippians 1 show his fondness:

I thank my God every time I remember you (v. 3).

In all my prayers for all of you, I always pray with joy because of your partnership in the gospel from the first day until now (vv. 4–5).

It is right for me to feel this way about all of you, since I have you in my heart . . . (v. 7).

God can testify how I long for all of you with the affection of Christ Jesus (v. 8).

These warm phrases show the depth of friendship Paul had with the Philippian believers. It's fair to say the letter to the Philippians is one of the most heartfelt letters Paul wrote. Undoubtedly, his being diverted, meeting Lydia, and experiencing the earthquake that led to the conversion of the Philippian jailer served to inspire the words Paul said during his later jail sentence. When he says, "What has happened to me has actually served to advance the gospel" (Philippians 1:12), he has the experience of what had happened to him in Philippi to give him the confidence that God is always in control. Paul knew God had a purpose for what was happening at the time of writing the letter to the Philippians from jail, just as God did with sending him to Philippi. The Bibles we now hold show that Paul was right.

We learn from Paul that time is never lost—the only thing we might lose is what we wanted to do with it. Paul's many jail stays must have felt like a setback in spreading the gospel, and he could have looked at the time he spent in prison as a waste. But Paul believed God had him where he was for a reason, and he always looked at his circumstances for evidence that God was working. In the meantime, Paul took the time his prison sentence gave him and wrote letters to encourage churches, since he was unable to see them face-to-face.

Paul teaches us to trust that God is in every circumstance, and what we can't see now will one day add evidence to how God is working. It's incredible to think that without Paul's jail time, our Bibles might be very different from the ones we have. God uses circumstances we wouldn't choose to cause things to happen in the future that we can't imagine. The passing of time opens our eyes more and more to this truth.

Time eventually reveals that where we end up is right—no matter how different our path may have been from what we originally wanted. Time is our revealer, our teacher, and our encourager—and when we look back over how it was spent, God shows us what was happening that could not be seen. The passing of time encourages us to trust God *more*, and our faith is deepened as we see the multiple layers where God was working. We become encouraged that the paths we were led to were right, even if they led us away from where we wanted to be. Like Paul, we can proclaim that what is happening right now is somehow serving to advance God's purposes—even if we are in the dark about the ways God's purposes will continue to unfold.

In each of these three stories, we get a different truth about time that helps us recognize the way God works by how God uses it. Our time is always in God's hands. While knowing that doesn't take the struggle away, these stories give us enough evidence to hold on to in the midst of the struggle. Like Moses, we can trust God in our in-between times, knowing something is happening now that we might need in the future. When something feels too late, Abraham and Sarah show us that God is still able to fulfill our dreams despite our unbelief. The story of Paul and the Philippian church reveals that things that are constraining us right now may in time turn into a blessing we can't imagine. We see through these stories that time is never lost, even if what we wanted to do is not what we did.

Perhaps the biggest gift that time gives to our faith comes in the verse spoken by the three visitors who tell Abraham and Sarah that they will still have a child. My husband and I put this verse on the back of our wedding program because after all the time and brokenness of our backstories, it perfectly captured the way we felt.

Is anything too hard for the Lord?

Genesis 18:14

Long waits and interrupted plans make us feel the answer to that question is *yes*, because we've lived so many days in disappointment. However, when time finally reveals what it has been holding for us, this question turns into an exclamation and becomes the theme song of our faith.

REFLECTION QUESTIONS

1. Looking at Moses's chapter of running away to the wilderness (Exodus 2:15–25), have you ever looked back and seen the value of a season that seemed, when it was happening, to be meaningless time? If so, when was it? What do you see about it now?

2. Is there anything about Abraham's story in Genesis 17 that resonates with you? Do you have any prayer or hope that you've given up waiting for because it's taking too long? What in this passage encourages you?

3. Does Paul's story with the Philippian church in Acts 16 speak to any of your circumstances? Have you ever been led somewhere you didn't plan to go and been grateful later on? If so, when?

3

Forcing Your Way Can Complicate Your Life

"LET GO AND LET GOD" is a mantra many people put before themselves as a screen saver or wall hanging. "Move God out of the way and take over" isn't as popular, but it may be a better reflection of the way we live our lives. It's not easy to wait for a God whose ways and timing are so very different from ours.

There is a verse in Psalm 119 that begins with these words: "Though I constantly take my life in my hands . . ." (v. 109). I usually interrupt the sentence and stop there, because that phrase leaps off the page. Maybe you don't struggle with control (please mentor me), but this is the ongoing wrestling match of my life. The sentence finishes with "I will not forget your law," which is a declaration of the psalmist's intention. But the pull to take control from God is strong—and the word "constantly" shows how frequently this struggle takes place. If you connect with the sentiments of this verse, this chapter is for you.

It strikes me that a measure of growth in our lives happens after we turn sixteen, get into the driver's seat of a car, and start driving. A measure of growth in our spiritual lives happens the day we move into the passenger seat and let God drive our car. It's not hard to imagine why we resist giving up the autonomy we've attained. Especially when God is trying to lead us somewhere very different—at a much slower pace—than where we want to go.

> Our acceptance or resistance to the way God leads will set the course for the way we live our life.

Life with God is a partnership, and we have control of our part in the relationship. We aren't passive passengers in God's car; when we see where God is (or isn't) leading us, we get to control our response. Most of the time, the way God leads us is "along the way," which means that our response isn't a one-time decision. We continue to choose throughout our lives whether we will go at the pace—or in the direction—God leads. Our commitment to follow becomes complicated when God seems to stall, head down a detour, or take us somewhere we don't want to go.

It's been comforting for me to discover that people in the Bible also pushed against God's leading. These three stories encourage us that no matter how crazy or hard the path looks, the wise response is to trust. Our acceptance or resistance to the way God leads will set the course for the way we live our life.

GENESIS 32: What You Do Comes Back to You

Years ago, I spent a month by myself in Paris, and when I wandered into a church called Saint-Sulpice I was utterly captivated by a dimly lit painting. There were many beautiful paintings hanging in that church, but the one titled *Jacob Wrestling with the Angel* by Eugène Delacroix took my breath away. The artist painted Jacob with his head buried in the angel's chest, utterly engrossed in fighting him. What pulled me in was the way the winged figure was looking at Jacob—his eyes were fixed on his head, his arm was outstretched, and it appeared as if he were trying to lead him in a dance. I stood there silently pondering if I was looking at an allegory of my life.

Jacob was born with a prophecy that his older brother would one day serve him. His mother, Rebekah, heard this prophecy before her twin sons even arrived (Genesis 25:23). Jacob's name meant "he grasps the heel" or "deceiver," which gives us a foreshadowing of Jacob's personality. The fact that he was born grabbing his brother's heel as they came out of the womb gives us the first sign that Jacob might have trouble waiting for his life to play out.

Jacob moves from grasping his brother Esau's heel to outright manipulating him to give Jacob his birthright. He waits until Esau is starved, then holds a meal in front of him as a trade. Esau's belly prevents him from thinking clearly, and he throws away his birthright in a glib agreement. Though Esau acts carelessly, this scene reveals the moment that Jacob's manipulative behavior starts to rear its head. His scheming tendencies lead to an even bigger deception in Genesis 27, orchestrated by Rebekah, to fool his father, Isaac, into blessing him. Jacob dresses up like Esau and tricks his nearly blind father into giving him Esau's firstborn blessing instead. The birthright may have been Jacob's destiny, but the way that destiny came about seemed to be a little more Jacob than God.

Esau is, of course, furious—which prompts Jacob to run away and live with an uncle who seems to be no accident in Jacob's journey. Uncle Laban may even be slightly more advanced in his ability to deceive. This is apparent when Jacob agrees to work seven years to marry Laban's daughter Rachel, then (with veils and lots of wine) somehow ends up marrying Rachel's sister, Leah. Jacob wakes up from consummating his marriage with his veiled bride and discovers Leah in his bed. When Jacob cries out to Laban, "Why have you deceived me?" (Genesis 29:25), we wonder if Esau's words to him surfaced in his memory. The most effective way for God to confront our shortcomings is to allow us to see them in someone else. It seems God had purpose in placing Uncle Laban in Jacob's life.

During his time with Laban, Jacob moves from deceiver to deceived, and in this chapter of his life, God begins smoothing his rough edges. Laban tells Jacob if he works seven *more* years he can marry Rachel too; so, fourteen years and multiple wives later, Jacob finally gets the love of his life. Needless to say, it's a bit more crowded in Jacob's household than he originally bargained for, and the complications of these relationships (including the twelve sons and one daughter that came from them) serve to work on Jacob's character. These relationships give him many more chances to learn the lesson of acceptance for the rest of his life.

It's worth noticing that after Jacob took God's plan into his hands, Jacob's plan was subsequently taken from him. His plan to marry Rachel didn't happen the way he wanted, and this was the first time Jacob experienced something that wasn't in his control. The parallel between the relationship of Jacob and Esau and that of Laban and Jacob can't be missed, because it reveals something important about the way God works both *in* and *through* us. God's ultimate plan for Jacob to carry the birthright isn't thwarted, but this episode of Jacob's life shows that our flaws are not overlooked. Instead, God often allows frustrating circumstances and difficult relationships to refine us. Laban is in Jacob's life to help Jacob see himself.

In Genesis 32, Jacob finally moves his family away from Laban's home, and he decides to send messengers to see if he can make peace with Esau. But that desire for peace is choked by terror when he finds out that his long-estranged brother is coming his way. Jacob initially tries to keep Esau at bay with an offering, but as Esau moves closer, Jacob has no control over what will happen. We can only imagine (as does Jacob) that the years have increased Esau's rage. I love the way Genesis 32 is written, because it builds suspense for what Esau might be feeling. We read that he has four hundred men and is headed toward Jacob (v. 6), but we don't know his intention, because the chapter focuses on Jacob's thoughts. All of this buildup brings us to the passage where Jacob's control issues come to their culminating fight. Jacob's lifelong wrestling reaches a climax when he enters the ring with an angel of God.

This passage (Genesis 32:22–30) is both famous and mysterious; in a dreamlike sequence, Jacob wrestles someone who appears to be half man, half angel. Even stranger, the figure Jacob wrestles—who Jacob later refers to as God—is the first to call the fight. Yet Jacob is the one who leaves the wrestling match with a limp.

When the heavenly figure tells Jacob to let him go, Jacob utters these bold words: "I will not let you go unless you bless me" (Genesis 32:26).

I find it curious that after Jacob makes this request, the angel asks him to state his name. Jacob has to say out loud, "My name is 'Grasping the heel, Deceiver'" (see v. 27), to which the angel replies, in so many words, "You will no longer have that name."

Here's the way the verse reads: "Your name will no longer be Jacob, but Israel, because you have struggled with God and with humans and have overcome" (Genesis 32:28).

We can't help but ask this question: if Jacob is the one left with the limp, what exactly has he overcome?

Perhaps the angel is referring to a different kind of over-coming than beating God in a wrestling match. Maybe what Jacob has overcome is the manipulation inside himself. From here on out in Jacob's story, he appears softer, and his life seems to be marked with more trust and obedience. The nation of Israel that will come forth through his twelve sons will carry Jacob's lesson because they will bear his new name.

The next morning, Jacob faces Esau, and this marks the first time in his story that he has to lean on God to orchestrate what will happen. His bribes and plans are no longer there to protect him; Jacob will have to let God lead him to face his past. From this moment forward, Jacob will limp with God's help throughout his life.

The winged figure in the painting in Paris has always depicted for me what a struggle with control looks like. God looks lovingly upon our striving and then takes our hand to lead us through life's dance. We welcome following God when we are being led to places of joy and satisfaction. God's dance becomes harder to follow when we are given a diagnosis, or our income doesn't cover what we need. If you are like Jacob (and me), that's when you push your head against God's chest because you don't like the dance that is happening. But God whispers, "Let me lead you through the hard, because I have a plan that is beyond what you now know. If you give in and let me lead you, I will take you to places that you will never be able to go on your own."

Through Jacob's wrestling match in Genesis 32, we discover that God has grace for controllers. Our limps help us see our dependence and recognize what little control we actually have. As Jacob's story progresses, we find that the older Jacob is more mellow than the younger Jacob. He is less manipulative, gentler, the edges of his personality more refined. When Esau comes running toward him in Genesis 33,

Jacob gets his first taste of wonder at God's ability to bring the unexpected. As Jacob's sons grow up and one of them ends up becoming a ruler in Egypt, Jacob will continue to experience more of God's surprises. When we stop wrestling God for control, we can let God lead us in life's unimaginable dance.

From Jacob's story we discover that the limp doesn't just come alongside a blessing; it is part of it. When we have learned dependence, we more willingly move from the driver's seat to the passenger seat and let God run our life.

1 SAMUEL 15: Compromise Is a Subtle Detour

Compromise is a subtle detour. It begins with a very slight turn and slowly leads you off course. For King Saul that turn began when he let his insecurity convince him that people-pleasing was the way to gain followers. He couldn't see the dilemma that trying to gain followers puts your followers in charge. What is true in the world of social media was also true for Saul in his kingdom. Your leadership and influence diminish if the people you are leading end up leading you.

When King Saul is introduced in 1 Samuel 9, we get the first hint of his insecurity. Other leaders in the Bible start out with some insecurity, but unfortunately for Saul, he feeds this insecurity until it defines his life. The way he appears in front of others is more important than his calling. You can see it when Samuel tells Saul he will be a leader in Israel's future, and this is his response:

> But am I not a Benjamite, from the smallest tribe of Israel, and is not my clan the least of all the clans of the tribe of Benjamin? Why do you say such a thing to me?
>
> 1 Samuel 9:21

Other leaders, like Moses and Gideon, respond similarly at the beginning of their calling (see Exodus 3 and Judges 6). But unlike Gideon and Moses, Saul lets his insecurity overshadow God's direction and lead him on a downward path.

Before Saul's conquest of the Philistines, he is told to wait for Samuel for seven days to make an offering. On the seventh day, the troops start to get impatient, so Saul decides to do the offering before Samuel arrives (see 1 Samuel 13:8–9). When Samuel confronts him, instead of confessing his wrongdoing, Saul justifies his behavior, saying that if he had waited, his army would have left him. His path of leadership begins to move from insecurity into a pattern of excuses and lies. Though he is warned by Samuel where this kind of leadership will lead, Saul's compromises continue to chart his course.

After more battles and questionable leadership, 1 Samuel 15 marks the final time Saul is given instructions about what to do in the upcoming battle. Again Saul compromises—doing only part of what Samuel says. He can't resist allowing his men to preserve some things they are not supposed to keep in order to uphold his reputation and power. When Samuel comes to confront him for the last time, Saul has the audacity to greet him with these words: "The LORD bless you! I have carried out the LORD's instructions" (1 Samuel 15:13).

Saul has moved beyond disobedience to boldly rearranging the truth before Samuel even speaks to him. Saul's lie is compounded by his justification, claiming that the reason he kept what he wasn't supposed to keep was so he could make a bigger sacrifice to God. Saul rationalizes his actions with these words: "The soldiers brought them from the Amalekites; they spared the best of the sheep and cattle to sacrifice to the LORD your God" (1 Samuel 15:15).

By beginning with *the soldiers brought them,* Saul bypasses himself as the leader who had control of this wrongdoing. He admits what we already know: Saul's army, rather than Saul, is in charge. He then justifies himself by explaining that their motivation for not obeying was so that they could make a bigger sacrifice. However, notice that when Saul tells Samuel who the sacrifice was for, he refers to God as Samuel's Lord instead of his. It seems that Saul is inadvertently no longer aligning himself with God. People-pleasing has subtly and stealthily become Saul's lord.

Saul's demise leads him to desperation when he goes from lying about his disobedience to begging Samuel to forgive him (v. 25). Unfortunately, he makes it obvious in his confession that God's disapproval is not what Saul fears most. The god Saul fears is what people think of him, and he makes that clear when he says, "I was afraid of the men and so I gave in to them" (1 Samuel 15:24). The insecurity he felt when he first became king has grown with each act of disobedience as he tried to hold his reputation in place. Ironically, the thing Saul desperately tries to cling to eludes him more and more the harder he tries to hold on to it. When we let go and let God lead us, other things fall into their rightful place.

> The irony is, the more you make pleasing others your goal, the less likely it will be that you will achieve it.

"I was afraid of the men and so I gave in to them" is a sidebar warning for what can happen when we stop being who we are and try to be what others want from us. Social media makes it tempting to live for being noticed or for getting a big response. When we weigh ourselves by our followers, we are left with the weight of trying to please them. This takes our focus from living the life and plan that God has given us. The irony is, the more you make pleasing others your goal, the less likely it will

be that you will achieve it. The only audience who is consistent in loving us unconditionally is God.

Saul does finally admit he has blown it, but only after all other options have eluded him. In verse 25 he follows his confession with a request for Samuel to accompany him in front of his people, because he doesn't want to lose their respect. Samuel rejects Saul's request, and this leads Saul to grab and tear the edge of Samuel's robe, in a desperate attempt to force him (v. 27). Saul's action becomes a symbol Samuel uses to communicate that God is tearing the kingdom away from him, because Saul's allegiance to his ego outweighs his allegiance to God.

Saul begs Samuel a second time to go with him, saying in verse 30, "Please honor me before the elders of my people and before Israel." You resort to coercing people to honor you when no honor is deserved. Samuel concedes, but only after he makes it clear that Saul will no longer be the leader of God's kingdom. Samuel may have to comply with what the acting king requests of him, but neither he nor God will allow this continuing farce. From this point on, Saul's desperation for people's approval eventually turns into insanity. Because of Saul's decisions not to go the way God leads him, the course of his leadership moves him to madness, marked by mistrust, suspicion, and fear.

At the end of chapter 15, we find Samuel (and God) grieving about Saul's compromises. Saul's story continues, but this is how 1 Samuel 15:35 ends:

> Until the day Samuel died, he did not go to see Saul again, though Samuel mourned for him. And the Lord regretted that he had made Saul king over Israel.

It seems that sadness, rather than anger, is what God feels when we can't let go of something in order to follow Him. Letting go and letting God lead is how we live our best life.

Saul had the kingdom in front of him, but his irrepressible need for approval and admiration overruled God's leading. By continuing to pursue that need rather than God's direction, he ended up losing both. That's the sad irony of Saul's life, and the lesson we can take from his life into ours.

2 SAMUEL 11 and PSALM 51: Wrong Turns Can Become Your Testimony

Letting God lead is an ongoing decision in our faith journey. It's not a one-time choice; it's a thousand decisions we make every day throughout our life. There isn't a single person in the Bible (or world) who lives their whole life in perfect alignment with God's leading. What seems to be more important is your willingness to turn around when you've gone off God's path. Of all the decisions you make, the most important one is the one you make next.

David is described as "a man after [God's] own heart" before Samuel even meets him (1 Samuel 13:14). Saul was chosen for his kingly physical attributes, but David is chosen for his heart. When Samuel is sent to anoint David as king, God tells Samuel to look beyond the physical attributes of David's older brothers to choose him. David does eventually grow into a mighty warrior, but the Bible makes it clear that it was what was inside David that made him God's choice.

That's why it is particularly disturbing when David gets himself embroiled in a scene of catastrophic adultery. It's a warning that no matter how rock-solid we may feel, we are one temptation away from a terrible choice. David's avalanche of bad decisions begins when he is wandering on his rooftop listlessly and sees Bathsheba bathing. He is warned immediately that she is the wife of one of his soldiers, but David answers the warning with silence, which is the subtle indication that he won't be swayed from what he wants. The worst part about David's adultery is that Bathsheba's husband, Uriah, was one of his most loyal soldiers. While David is on his rooftop peering at (and eventually having sex with) Uriah's wife, Uriah is fighting a war on David's behalf. When David calls him back from war to try to cover up Bathsheba's illicit pregnancy, Uriah refuses to sleep with her. Uriah can't indulge in a night of passion with his wife while his fellow soldiers are out fighting, and his integrity leaves David holding his mistake. David remains on his downward spiral when he covers up his sin by ordering Uriah to be placed on the front lines of battle. Uriah is subsequently killed, and the last verse in 2 Samuel 11 states the obvious truth that lurks in David's heart: "The thing David had done displeased the LORD" (v. 27).

It's hard to imagine how David got to this point, but somehow he was able to drown out God's voice long enough to silence Him. The beautiful truth of God's grace is that even then, God doesn't give up. God sends Nathan the prophet to David, and Nathan tells David a story. It's a sad tale meant to be an allegory about a rich man who has plenty of sheep and cattle but decides to take the only lamb of a poor man and cook it for a guest. David becomes incensed and shouts that the man deserves to die, and it's not hard to imagine how Nathan must have looked at him. David's reckoning comes packaged in the words that Nathan says next: "You are the man!" (2 Samuel 12:7).

The next decision David makes is the best decision of his life: he takes full ownership of his actions. This marks a difference between him and Saul—when David is confronted, he immediately repents. The word *repent* is not just a word from a fanatic's sign or social media post, it's the willingness to turn around and go in a different direction. In Hebrew, the word is translated "to change one's mind," which is directional; it's not just feeling bad about what you did. Repentance is more than remorse; it is recommitting to let God lead *and* being willing to follow Him. Though David and Saul both say, "I have sinned," only David follows his confession with actions that prove his remorse. Turning around and walking in a new direction is what you need to do to change your course.

If David was still able to turn around after his adultery and indirect murder, we can all have hope that we are never beyond God's forgiveness. This chapter of David's life demonstrates that the size of your sin isn't what determines God's grace. No matter how far we've wandered off God's path, David shows us that we are only a decision away from realignment. David's decision to turn back and boldly accept God's grace gives all strayers hope.

> Wrong turns may complicate our life, but they also offer us a calling to be a channel of God's grace.

Psalm 51 is David's prayer after Nathan's confrontation. It's a prayer that has been repeated in thousands of churches (including mine) by countless sinners (including me) many times since. The words of Psalm 51 are an example of how God can redeem wrong turns by taking what we learned from them and using it to help others. Wrong turns may complicate our life, but they also offer us a calling to be a channel of God's grace.

A couple of things we shouldn't overlook in this psalm—David begins, "Have mercy on me, O God, according to your unfailing love" (v. 1), because he boldly believes that God's love will be the judge that decides the outcome of his confession. God's grace is given because of God's love. This is good news for any of us who feel our sin negates the grace that's available to us; according to this line, grace is not a quid pro quo agreement. David can't earn God's mercy even if he tried, because God's unfailing love is the source.

It's interesting that David says, "Against you, you only, have I sinned" (v. 4), when his sin was also against Bathsheba and Uriah. In the original language of the text, the Hebrew word for *only* can mean alone, but it could also mean branch or part. This leaves room for the understanding that David's confession to God was one branch or part of his admission of wrongdoing. The most important thing to notice is that David takes full ownership of what he did.

If you've ever received an apology filled with excuses, you know how it minimizes the apology. Excuses change the apology's tone, lessening the apologizer's responsibility and minimizing the remorse. David models the courage to hold your own blame—which opens the door wide for God to meet it with His grace.

In verse 10, David asks God to "renew a steadfast spirit" within him, showing that he wants to reinstate his course in following Him. David wants not only to get back to where he was but to *stay* on his previous path. His wrong turn broadened his map with a detour, but it doesn't have to change his trajectory. Grace will recalculate his tragic mistake and use it in David's life.

David shows that he wants God to rebuild the resolute spirit he once had, so that in the future he will respond differently to God's leading. After experiencing the tragic result of going the way he thought he wanted, he wants to realign himself with God's course. The word *steadfast* means loyal, faithful, and resolute; David doesn't ever want to return to where his immediate desires led him. Short-term gratification was the road that failed him; now he is ready to go through short-term denial for long-term joy and peace.

Following God away from something we desperately want requires more than trust—it requires a willingness to submit when we don't feel like it. There are times when God's ways, timing, and withholding don't make sense. When David says, "Grant me a willing spirit, to sustain me" (v. 12), he knows his immediate desires will continue to coax him. He will have to be willing to let God lead him away from something he wants, but he now knows that only his compliance will sustain and satisfy his heart. He has experienced what happens when he pushes God aside and follows what he thinks will fulfill him. A night of passion was hardly worth the pain he inflicted on Uriah and Bathsheba, not to mention the guilt and remorse he brought into his life.

David's prayer for a willing spirit reaffirms that obedience is a choice—a choice that demands more from us when it appears God is withholding something. When David wanted Bathsheba, he couldn't see past what he wanted to what it would become. God sees what we can't see, but He gives us the freedom to choose to trust Him. David's pain from going his own way convinced him that a willing spirit would help him lean on God's long-term vision when he couldn't see.

The word of hope from David's life is that we are never too far to turn back.

David proclaims his new mission: to teach transgressors God's ways and help sinners turn back to the God who saved him (vv. 13–14). This mission comes from the only gift his wrong turn gave him: he now has a visceral understanding of God's grace. If he could have a do-over in his decisions with Bathsheba, my guess is that David would take it. In 2 Samuel 12:24, when David has to comfort Bathsheba in the loss that he was responsible for, it's hard to imagine the depth of his grief. Wrong turns can't be taken back, but they can be used as warning signs for when we are tempted to push God aside in our journey. The word of hope from David's life is that we are never too far to turn back.

Forcing our way may complicate our life, but wrong turns can become our testimony. After a wrong turn, we are filled with a new resolve to trust God's way, even when God's direction or pace conflicts with what we want. When we are tempted to pursue an immediate need or desire, our experience with wrong turns makes us more likely to see through the temptation. The stories of these three men show that God doesn't take authority over our actions without our participation; we need to put our hand in God's and continue staying the course. Jacob, Saul, and David show us that a willing spirit is what matters most, even if we have to wrestle with God or take a wrong turn to find it. The most important decision after taking things into our own hands is the decision we make next.

REFLECTION QUESTIONS

1. Looking at Jacob's story with Laban in Genesis 29, has God ever put a person in your life to show you something about yourself? If so, who was it and what did you learn?

2. When you observe Saul's compromises in 1 Samuel 15, what stands out to you? Is there anything about his behavior that resonates with something you've done or felt? If so, what does this passage teach you?

3. Looking from 2 Samuel 11–12 to Psalm 51, you can see David's remorse for what he did with Bathsheba. Have you ever made a mistake that God used in your life? What does David's story show you about the decision we make after a bad decision?

4

Your Little Leads to God's Big

WHEN I ASKED HER IF IT WAS OKAY if I picked her up from school once a week, she smiled shyly and nodded. I couldn't have imagined where that nod would lead. I didn't have a clue what we would *do* together; her world was beyond my experience. All I knew was that I was pulled by a tug from God to invite myself into her life.

We met at a children's after-school program in downtown Los Angeles on 6th and San Pedro. I was a volunteer on Tuesdays to help organize activities for kids on Skid Row—kids whose parents lived in hotels or on the streets. She came into my focus because of her understated personality and captivating smile. Her spirit drew me in, but I felt her life needed more than I had. Apparently God felt differently, because that tug wouldn't go away until I finally tiptoed into a relationship that changed my life.

My small step grew into a friendship and eventual mentorship that allowed me to be a midwife to a miracle. Through this girl, I was able to participate in one of the great stories of my life. She ended up spending holidays with my family, got through junior high and high school while living in her dad's hotel room, and frequently had to share her living space with prostitutes. During her sophomore year she found out at a doctor's appointment that she was pregnant and bravely made the decision to give her baby up. She wanted her child to have the chance for a life that she didn't have.

We visited adoption agencies and pored over books to choose the couple. After she made her choice, her baby boy was born three weeks early and the couple decided they wanted a girl, so the adoption fell through. I drove to the hospital on the day of his birth and prayed over his tiny body. The next day I helped to get him into temporary foster care until we could figure out our next move. Days later, my best friend told me about a couple who taught at her kids' school—and they had been trying desperately for seven years to have a child. My girl and I drove down to their house to meet them, and with a high five and a yes, she decided this was the couple who could give her baby a home. It's been eighteen years since that day, and that three-week-old baby I prayed over went to college last year on a basketball scholarship. His parents and I still stay in touch, and I continue to marvel at the unimaginable story God wrote.

It turns out one step is all God needs to change a destiny. Stories in the Bible (and ours) reveal that the opportunity in front of us may end up being a bigger decision than we know. On the brink of that decision, we may battle fear, lack of knowledge, and overwhelming incompetence. But if we are willing to step out anyway, we may get a front-row seat to wonder, which is worth the fight.

In the passages that follow, we'll look at the decisions that three people made without knowing what would happen because of them. They illustrate the profound truth that we might be on the verge of a story we would never *not* choose, if only we could see what was ahead. That stirring in your heart, the turned-up volume of a person's voice, the strange timing of an opportunity—each of these is used by God to beckon you into an unknown destiny. Faith is responding to what is in front of you and trusting God's purpose for what it will be.

> **Faith is responding to what is in front of you and trusting God's purpose for what it will be.**

RUTH 1: A Small Path Can Lead to a Big Path

The book of Ruth is a small story of two women coping with tragedy. Sandwiched between the books of Judges and 1 Samuel, it's the story of how a young woman and her mother-in-law overcome their tragedy and end up joining their lives. There may be no other book that more clearly depicts how a choice in front of you could end up being the turning point that defines your life.

The book opens at the end of a heartbreaking turn of events. Naomi had moved to Moab with her husband and two sons, and after both her sons marry, all three women end up losing their husbands. All of this happens at the beginning of chapter one, so this book immediately gives the insight that if tragedy strikes and we are still here, God must have another chapter for us ahead. Naomi is left alone with her two daughters-in-law, and because she's an Israelite and they are Moabites, she tells them to go back to their families. She has decided to go back to her family because she has no relatives in Moab, and as a single woman, she has to find support. Naomi is clearly adored by both her daughters-in-law, because neither of them wants to leave her. After Naomi tries to convince them to go back to their home, Ruth declares she will not leave her side. Here is what Ruth says:

> Don't urge me to leave you or to turn back from you. Where you go I will go, and where you stay I will stay. Your people will be my people and your God my God. Where you die I will die, and there I will be buried. May the LORD deal with me, be it ever so severely, if even death separates you and me.
>
> Ruth 1:16–17

You may have heard these words at a wedding and not known they were words from a daughter-in-law to her mother-in-law. It's an encouragement to all mothers-in-law that it's possible to smash a stereotype—Naomi was not tolerated, she was beloved. But Ruth's words show that something more has drawn her to join lives with her mother-in-law. It is more than her affection for her, it is an attraction to her mother-in-law's faith. Scripture is silent about what drew Ruth to Naomi's faith, but we can see that allegiance to Naomi's God is a part of Ruth's commitment to her. Her promise turns into a confession of faith when she says, "Your people will be my people and your God my God" (v. 16). In verse 17, she even refers to Naomi's God as "the LORD"—indicating the possibility that Ruth has already embraced Naomi's God as her own.

Ruth begins her statement of commitment by saying, "Don't urge me to leave you or to turn back from you" (v. 16), which is a plea for Naomi to stop arguing with Ruth about why she shouldn't stay with her. Sometimes we have to prevail against the reasons people might give us for holding back from what we feel called to do—especially when those reasons are good. Looking back in the passage, when Naomi is telling her daughters-in-law why they should leave her, she gives them these despairing words:

> Return home, my daughters. Why would you come with me? Am I going to have any more sons, who could become your husbands? Return home, my daughters; I am too old to have another husband.
>
> Ruth 1:11–12

Clearly the reasons *not* to follow Naomi are compelling, especially to newly widowed women, who are the poorest group in this culture. Because of the desperate circumstances they all now face, Ruth has to close her ears to Naomi's words so she won't be dissuaded from her call. Naomi takes it a step further in verse 13, saying they will grow old waiting to marry if they stay with her, and that dire prediction is enough to convince Ruth's sister-in-law. Yet even with these ominous words about her future, Ruth will not be swayed to return home. In steps of faith, we need to stay focused on the path God is calling us to, rather than the future that *might* be ahead. If you've been walking with God long enough, you know that what "might be ahead" rarely is.

When I was called to a church in Santa Barbara right after I went through the broken engagement, someone warned me just before I moved that there were no single people living in that city. They referred to it as "a place for the newly wed and nearly dead," and as a single woman, let's just say this was not exactly a hopeful prediction about my new home. Twelve years after marrying my husband in Santa Barbara, I sit here writing and think back to what my life would be like if I had heeded that warning. The man I married, the boy I raised, and the church I served are all a part of my life because I did not.

Naomi reveals her despondency about her dark chapter of faith when she says, "the LORD's hand has turned against me" (v. 13) and *still* Ruth makes her commitment to stay with her. Naomi may be in a season where she can't see God's hand, but Ruth obviously sees past that to what she has previously witnessed from Naomi's faith. Ruth's declaration shows that despite what Naomi currently feels her God is doing to her, Ruth still wants Naomi's God to be her God too.

So even in the middle of Naomi's dark chapter of faith, Ruth declares her commitment to take on the God who has disappointed them. Something in Ruth is able to look beyond Naomi's disillusionment and commit herself to the God she has experienced from Naomi's life. It's comforting to know that even in the dark parts of our stories, God can woo others to belief.

The two women leave together for Naomi's home, which happens to be in Bethlehem in Judah. Hundreds of years later, a young couple will be passing through this same city, and in a barn with a manger, they will give birth to the Son of God. Ruth could never have imagined when she made her commitment to go with Naomi how significant Naomi's town would be in her faith's future. The geographical details of this story reveal the way God weaves His bigger plan with the smaller plans of our lives. One day Ruth would take her place in the lineage of Jesus, and her new hometown would be the place He was born.

Looking back to Naomi's words that there will be no hope for a husband if Ruth follows her, we can marvel once more about God loving to do the impossible. Not only did Ruth eventually marry a wonderful man named Boaz, but it's likely he had a special heart for foreigners because (as you saw in an earlier chapter) Rahab was his mom. Ruth walked into a story that seemed orchestrated just for her, but she had to take that step of faith to find it. By following Naomi to offer her companionship and help her with provisions, Ruth was noticed by a man who saw how she took care of Naomi, and he was drawn to her beautiful heart. Sometimes the path for our future comes through saying yes to the need on our path.

And what about Naomi? Her words of doubt about the future she imagined in her grief turned into words of triumph. Her sadness was redeemed through the daughter-in-law who would not leave her side. Through Ruth's romance with Naomi's relative, Naomi experienced new joy in the birth of Ruth's child. That child was named Obed, and in the brief genealogy at the end of Ruth, we discover David's grandfather was Ruth's son. Many generations later in Matthew 1, we discover Ruth's child was part of an even longer line that brought the Son of God.

> Sometimes the path for our future comes through saying yes to the need on our path.

The story of two women coming together to find a life beyond their dreams is a testament to how God writes His big story from our small stories. We are called to make decisions on the path in front of us; God orchestrates where that path leads. Sometimes the step of faith we are invited to take feels too big—and it may come packaged with compelling reasons not to take it. But if we trust God for the pull we feel to step out anyway, God loves to surprise us with what that step becomes.

1 SAMUEL 25: A Step of Faith Can Change Destiny

Steps of faith usually include risk, and there is often a limited time to make your decision. You have to focus on what you know—rather than what might happen—to decide whether or not to proceed. Ruth's decision to care for Naomi ended up being life-changing, but Ruth didn't see that when she decided to follow her mother-in-law. The important thing is that she didn't let the fear of what *might* happen hold her back from moving ahead.

Keeping our eyes on the things we know rather than what we don't know helps us discern whether to move forward in a decision. This is especially important when we have a short window of time before the opportunity is gone. The story of Abigail shows how to balance discernment with courage, which is needed when taking a risk.

When Abigail and her husband, Nabal, are introduced, we can see that even though they were married, they had different reputations. First Samuel 25:3 says, "She was an intelligent and beautiful woman, but her husband was surly and mean in his dealings"—so it seems Abigail might have been stuck in a marriage she tolerated because she had no choice. Because the husband had the controlling voice of the household, Abigail had likely been a victim of her husband's "mean dealings" throughout her married life.

The specific "mean dealing" we hear about in this chapter was a run-in between Nabal and David's men, who were asking for a return favor for protecting Nabal's servants. Because David's men had provided for Nabal's men while they were in the wilderness, David asked Nabal if he would do the same for his men now that they were on Nabal's land. Here was Nabal's message back:

Who is this David? Who is this son of Jesse? . . . Why should I take my bread and water, and the meat I have slaughtered for my shearers, and give it to men coming from who knows where?

1 Samuel 25:10–11

You can imagine David's response.

One of the servants immediately tells Abigail about Nabal's message, which indicates that Abigail is respected more than her husband for her discernment and influence. In a culture of dominating males, Abigail seems to be seen by those around her as the true leader of this house. The servant tells Abigail that David's men had fiercely protected them when they were in the wilderness, so she should act quickly to intervene in Nabal's message back to David. The servant ends his message with these words:

> Now think it over and see what you can do, because disaster is hanging over our master and his whole household. He is such a wicked man that no one can talk to him.
>
> 1 Samuel 25:17

Trusting Abigail to make the right decision, the servant ends his plea by asking her to ponder everything he's told her. Abigail's wicked and unreasonable husband has represented more people than himself; now the whole household is in danger because of his response. Taking action involves huge risk to Abigail on two accounts—first, she has no idea how David will receive her, and second, she doesn't know what Nabal will do to her if he finds out. Abigail has to decide whether the opportunity in front of her is a calling that is worth the risk.

Decisions that involve risk often have to be made fast—we don't get much time to think them over. Sometimes we miss the window of what we are called to do because we take too long to decide. When it comes to these decisions, it's helpful to remember that making *no decision* is actually a decision. We can tell ourselves we are putting the decision off, but the opportunity might not still be there if we take too long. If Abigail had waited, the chance she had to help her household would have been gone.

Verse 18 says, "Abigail acted quickly"—she sees her chance to intervene and knows she is the one called to do it. She quickly packs the provisions David had asked for and leaves to face David with her servants' help. When she gets to David, even though she is a wealthy landowner's wife, she bows humbly before him. She is direct about her husband's foolish behavior, and she is wise enough to appeal to David's faith not to take revenge. She reminds him that taking revenge would impact not just his relationship with Nabal but his relationship with God, which she knew of by David's reputation. She ends her plea with these compelling words:

> When the LORD has fulfilled for my lord every good thing he promised concerning him and has appointed him ruler over Israel, my lord will not have on his conscience the staggering burden of needless bloodshed or of having avenged himself. And when the LORD your God has brought my lord success, remember your servant.
>
> 1 Samuel 25:30–31

This foolish landowner's wise wife speaks straight to David's heart, and he is immediately pacified. His anger toward Nabal is subdued by Abigail's forthright wisdom to let God be in control of his revenge. Here's how he responds:

> Praise be to the LORD, the God of Israel, who has sent you today to meet me. May you be blessed for your good judgment and for keeping me from bloodshed this day and from avenging myself with my own hands.
>
> 1 Samuel 25:32–33

It's interesting that after taking this risk to humbly confront him, Abigail is praised by David for her good judgment. She seized her opportunity to speak to David honestly because she knew he was a man of great faith, and she trusted his response.

By acting on what she knew, Abigail could trust God with what she didn't know, and that showed great discernment. What God did with her words was up to God—and as usual, it was more than she knew.

Her words not only intervened on behalf of her household, they touched David's heart and made a lasting impression. God infused Abigail's words with a power that was beyond her control. Abigail's risk allowed God to use her, and with that risk, God made a pathway to a new future. But she had to step out not knowing how, or if, she would be used.

Abigail's conversation with David eventually led to a new chapter in her life, but there is also evidence that the experience of stepping out in faith changed her. After she returned from her conversation with David, she boldly told her husband what she had done and "his heart failed him"—then ten days later, he died (1 Samuel 25:37–38). Note the difference in Abigail from verse 19 to verse 37; she moves from sneaking around him to confronting him directly. She is no longer captive to any fear of her husband; her courage seems to have grown from her bold act.

> That is the interesting truth about fear and courage: whichever one you feed grows greater.

That is the interesting truth about fear and courage: whichever one you feed grows greater. The more we shrink back from risks, the more we feed our fear, but an act of courage can embolden our faith.

At the end of the chapter, David hears that Abigail is widowed and invites her to marry him. It's clear from verse 33 that it was Abigail's courage and good judgment that had attracted David most. So Abigail's decision to take a risk not only changed her household's fate, it brought her a new chapter.

But she had to step out in faith before she saw how things would unfold.

With Abigail, we see from a different angle how the opportunities in front of us can unfold big outcomes. Looking back over her story, we can see that her future was embedded in her risk. Maybe yours is too.

JOHN 6: What You Have Is All God Needs

From a decision to leave your home, to the risk of intervening before a disaster, to giving God . . . your lunch? This story is the perfect way to end this chapter for those who might feel what you have is too little for God to use. Maybe you are a bit intimidated by the steps of faith you just read about in Ruth and Abigail. The miracle of what God does with a lunch will show that the little you think you have is all God needs.

It's easy to feel that we don't have what it takes for God to use us. When it comes to faith, *not having what it takes* is exactly what God needs. The space between what you have and what God does with it is the space where God loves to shine.

The feeding of the five thousand is one of the only stories of Jesus's ministry that's recorded in all four gospels. However, John 6 gives us the detail I want to focus on—in this passage we discover the backstory of the food that Jesus used. The rest of the accounts include the lunch itself—five loaves and two fishes—but John tells us where the food originated. We learn from verse 9 that the loaves and fishes came from one boy's lunch.

Looking closely at the text, we can't be sure how this boy volunteered for his food to be taken. What we do know is that the boy must have made his food known, and when Andrew saw this, he offered what the boy had to Jesus. I'm guessing the boy thought others in the crowd would do the same, and he might have been waiting for the pile of food that would be accumulated. I can't imagine how this boy felt when his food was all there was, and he and his lunch took center stage.

Andrew states the obvious: "Here is a boy with five small barley loaves and two small fish, but how far will they go among so many?" (John 6:9). Now all eyes are on this boy's food, and the only thing the boy knows for sure is that he no longer has his lunch. The amount of food was minimal, so the boy might have been wondering what in the world Jesus would do with it. He may also have been wondering what he would say when his mother asked, "How was your lunch?"

When Andrew says to Jesus, "Here is a boy," the eyes of the crowd must have shifted toward him. With five thousand men in attendance, and women and children not counted in that number, the sea of people now watching him extended beyond where he could see.

The boy is standing alongside the teacher everyone came to hear, so whatever Jesus does next will happen right in front of him. Suddenly he is a key player in the drama that is unfolding; he is no longer a bystander in the crowd. Scripture is silent about what might have transpired between Jesus and this boy, but given the way Jesus welcomed children in His ministry, I picture Jesus putting His arm around him. Maybe they even had a moment where they exchanged glances, and Jesus gave him a little wink. Whatever happened in that moment, we know from the passage that this boy was about to experience something he'd never forget.

The moments before this miracle occurred reveal the risk it takes to offer what we have before we know what will happen. Once more we see the same theme that we saw in the last two passages: we have to step out in faith *before* we see what God will do. For Ruth it was letting go of her home, for Abigail it was letting go of her security, and for this boy it meant letting go of his provision. Like everyone else there, the boy was hungry, but unlike everyone else, he had the means to satisfy himself. He had to release what he had to see what Jesus would do with it. If Jesus was not dissuaded by the little that he had to give Him, what he had could be used. The size of what we have does not hold God back—only the unwillingness to give up what we have.

In verse 10, Jesus says, "Have the people sit down," presumably setting the stage for what is about to happen. I imagine the boy was feeling more excited in the shadow of Jesus's confidence—it seemed like Jesus was getting people prepared for something that was ahead. Jesus takes the boy's loaves and fishes in His hands, gives thanks to God, and suddenly asks His disciples to pass out the food to thousands of people. How the boy's eyes must have grown when he saw his food multiply to satisfy every person who was there. I love to think about what Jesus might have said to the boy when he saw his lunch turn into a miracle. No gospel records that conversation, but what is recorded is what Jesus said after the miracle took place: "When they had all had enough to eat, he said to his disciples, 'Gather the pieces that are left over. Let nothing be wasted'" (John 6:12).

That was one directive the disciples never forgot.

When Jesus sends them out to gather the leftovers, they bring back twelve times as much as the boy had originally given Him. What Jesus ended up doing with the lunch shows what God can do with the little we have. The less there is of you, the bigger the space God has to work, and the more your faith grows when you see what God does.

This miracle put Jesus at the height of His popularity, and it likely changed that boy forever. Though he is nameless in John's gospel, and not even included in Matthew 14, Mark 6, and Luke 9, what is recorded in all four stories is the amount of food the boy gave. The fact that this amount is repeated in all four gospels emphasizes that the smallness of what we have is actually a key part of the miracle. The size of what we give does not limit what God can do; the only thing He needs is for us to let go of what we have.

Over and over God urges us to give Him what we've got and trust Him for what will happen with it. There may (and probably will) be hurdles in giving up our security or comfort, but the more we let go, the more we experience what God can do. It is also true that the more we give God to use, the more God grows our faith when we see what God does with it. And as the story of this boy illustrates, the greatest faith stories come not from what *we* do but what *God* does with us. The greater the space between what we've given God and what He does with it, the more God shines.

> The greater the space between what we've given God and what He does with it, the more God shines.

I experienced that when I said yes to befriending an inner-city girl I knew needed support and friendship. I felt I had little to offer her, but during the course of our relationship, God used what I had and gave me immeasurably more. I could never have imagined the irreplaceable stories that my decision to befriend her would unfold, but that is the space God fills when we say yes.

So often we look ahead in decisions of faith and try to assess whether we have what it takes to make the decision. Ruth, Abigail, and a boy with a lunch show us that looking ahead at what we think might happen will only constrain us in what we decide. When we try to guess the future, we cannot see all that God has planned in it. We have to trust that if we are called to step out and do what is in front of us, what we don't see will grow our faith.

Ruth made a decision to accompany her mother-in-law, and God used it to bring her to her destiny. Abigail took a risk to intervene and protect her household, and God used it to bring her a second chance at life. A boy gave all he had to eat to Jesus, and five thousand people experienced a miracle. None of these three could have imagined the things that would happen from the decisions they made.

Fear, comfort, and inadequacy keep many of us from giving what we have and letting God use it. They are obstacles to be sure, and we can spend our whole lives allowing them to cause us to miss out. The invitation God gives us is to move forward into the opportunity in front of us—even if all we see is the sacrifice. Past the obstacles and the sacrifice is a front-row seat to being stunned by the way God works.

REFLECTION QUESTIONS

1. Looking at Ruth 1, have you ever made a small-path decision that led to a big path for your life? Do you have any decision like that in front of you right now? How does Ruth's story inspire you?

2. How does the story of Abigail's courage in 1 Samuel 25 speak to you? Have you ever had to take a risk to make a courageous decision? Do you tend to take risks when it comes to your faith, or do you play it safe?

3. When you read the story of the boy in John 6, how does it affect your perspective of your resources? Have you ever felt hesitant to give what you have because you don't feel it's enough? Have you ever been afraid to let go of what you have for other reasons?

5

Guidance Comes
from Behind

THE WORD *REMEMBER* IS REPEATED in forty-seven verses, twenty-eight chapters, and nineteen books in the Bible.[1] Curiously, the word is most often used as a command or an encouragement for people who need assurance for what lies ahead. It seems strange that God would tell people to look back to find out how to move forward. But remembering God's faithfulness in the past is the way our faith is strengthened to lead us into what is to come.

Faith is being certain of what we do not see, so it stands to reason that living by faith is learning to live with unseen realities. When you are blind, you learn to navigate spaces you can't see by remembering what is there. The more we remember about things that are invisible to us, the more confident we

1. LearntheBible.org, Bible Concordance, s.v. "Remember," https://www.learn thebible.org/bible/concordance/19434.

are in the unseen spaces where we are functioning. Remembering is how blind people find a path forward that they can't see.

It's not hard to make the connection from physical blindness to walking by faith, and why God leads us spiritually through our memory. Disasters happen when we feed our imagination with what might be, instead of remembering all the ways that God has been there. Our fears turn into a self-fulfilling prophecy when we can't move forward because we convince ourselves of unseen obstacles. We don't lose what is ahead for us because God didn't have it there; we lose our faith to get there because of our fear.

Remembering is the armor we need to barrel our way through the unseen, because we know from past experience that God will carry us through whatever lies in front of us. Remembering is also how we do battle with doubt—and wondering how (or if) God will provide. Our trust grows through experiences of God's faithfulness, but faith can be nourished or starved by our memory. When we forget what God has done, we lose our hope for what God is able to do.

The stories that follow illustrate three different examples of how God leads us through our memory. They show how faith for the future is empowered or discouraged by the way we remember God's provision in the past. If you need faith for something that is coming, these passages reveal that the way to do it is to put a stake down in what God has done—write it, sing it, repeat it, and mark it boldly in your memory so you can regularly return to it. The places you return to in order to find God's faithfulness give you confidence for the places you will be led.

> When we forget what God has done, we lose our hope for what God is able to do.

GENESIS 35: **Go Back to Where God Met You**

Genesis 35 opens after a gruesome scene—a tragic invasion spearheaded by Jacob's sons left Jacob afraid of what would happen to them. Two of his twelve sons had led a deceitful massacre, and at the end of Genesis 34, Jacob is cowering from what might lie ahead. He is afraid that his household will be the target of an invasion, and he is outnumbered and unequipped for the forces he believes might be coming for them. Genesis 35:1 appears to open in the middle of a conversation between God and Jacob: "Then God said to Jacob, 'Go up to Bethel and settle there, and build an altar there to God, who appeared to you when you were fleeing from your brother Esau.'"

"Then God said" indicates that God's words to Jacob might be a response to something Jacob prayed before this chapter. God knows that Jacob is afraid about what might be coming, so God advises him where to go to face what might be ahead. These are interesting words for Jacob to hear when he's facing an unknown battle. Jacob is told to ready himself by returning to where God met him in the past. Jacob needs faith to face what might be in front of him, so God tells him to go back to the place where Jacob went before to receive the courage he needed. Going back to where God met him in the past will give him the faith he needs to face what might be ahead.

It was Jacob who named the place Bethel, which in Hebrew means "House of God," because that was where he first felt God's presence. Genesis 28:19 tells us Jacob actually renamed the city (originally called Luz), presumably to engrave it in his memory as a place where God lived. When Jacob met God there the first time, it was after he had gotten the birthright from his father and subsequently had to leave home because of his brother's anger. God met Jacob in a dream and assured him that He would be with him, and that gave Jacob the courage to move forward into the unknown. When he woke up from that original dream, Jacob marked the place with a stone pillar, then left to find his uncle and start his new family. Now, all these years later, he's here again—facing a new chapter of fear and uncertainty—because God told him to go back.

In our world, "house of God" is most often thought of as church—not because God exclusively lives there, but because it's where we return to remember God's faithfulness. Church is the place we revisit our own "stone pillars"—by singing songs and hearing Scripture to revitalize our faith. The reason we show up is not to check a box to try to earn God's favor; we go because we need a place to return to regularly to remember God's faithfulness. Our memory dims when we are trying to live out our faith on our own. We experience God in other believers, and this encourages us when we face fear and uncertainty in our own story. When we see how God is at work in others, we are reminded that God will be faithful to us too—even if we can't yet see what God will do. The "house of God" is the place we go to remember God lives—and in Genesis 35:1, that's where God tells Jacob to go to nourish his faith.

Jacob's response to what God tells him to do is worth noting—he tells everyone in his household to get rid of the foreign gods they are keeping. Before they return to the place where their faith will be nourished by God, they have to rid themselves of the gods they've gone to instead. For us today, the "gods" we've gone to are probably not idols, but things we've inadvertently worshiped by going to them for fulfillment. Whether it's food, alcohol, sex, social media followers, or whatever consumes our attention, it's easy to fill God's place with things we pursue to satisfy our restless heart. When Jacob cleans out his household of all other gods, we see our part in remembering. Before we can grow our faith for what is ahead, we have to reestablish *who* holds our faith.

After Jacob and his household arrive at Bethel, the next few paragraphs recall the litany of times when God met Jacob with faithfulness. First it was when Jacob was fleeing from his home (and especially his brother), but then in verse 9, Jacob is reminded of the time God met him after he left Laban's house. When he found out Esau was headed his way, he had an all-night wrestling match with an angel. That was the place God gave Jacob his limp and his blessing—and the angel gave Jacob a new name. From that point forward, he was no longer Jacob ("grasps the heel," "deceiver") but Israel—"struggles with God and overcomes" (Genesis 35:10), and that name was given to him just before he witnessed God's faithfulness in his reconciliation with Esau. These instances of God showing up in Jacob's life are all remembered here in Bethel, and in the "house of God," Jacob again finds strength to face what's ahead.

After recounting these past markers of faithfulness, God reiterates His promise of what He is going to do for Jacob. God tells him that a nation and a community of nations will come from his descendants, and then God repeats the promise He gave Jacob before: "The land I gave to Abraham and Isaac I also give to you, and I will give this land to your descendants after you" (Genesis 35:12).

This is the same promise Jacob got from God here before in Genesis 28:13–14; God repeats it to solidify it in his memory. After recounting every time God met Jacob in his past, God reiterates the promise of what He is going to do. God builds on the faithfulness Jacob has experienced before to help Jacob trust what God is promising to do in the future. Jacob can leave here unafraid of what others might do to him, because he's been strengthened by God.

Jacob comes to Bethel with his fear and leaves remembering God's faithfulness. Now he can face uncertainty ahead with the confidence he regained from his past. This passage

When we fear what's ahead, it's by remembering God's faithfulness in the past that we find our faith to move forward.

in Genesis 35 shows us that when we fear what's ahead, it's by remembering God's faithfulness in the past that we find our faith to move forward. Whether you do that at church, in your journal, or by regularly meeting with a friend who shares your faith, those touchstones are needed to remind us of God's invisible presence in our lives. By regularly refreshing our memory of who God has been for us, we can hold our faith for what God can do in the future. The opposite is also true; our spiritual amnesia can deplete our future faith.

The next passage illustrates how.

EXODUS 16: What You Remember Will Guide Your Faith

With the sound of whips and chains still ringing in their ears, the Israelites were told to stand back and watch God's deliverance. The eighty-year-old shepherd we left in Exodus 2 now holds out a giant stick in front of them and bellows God's commands. With the Egyptian army close on their heels, the Israelites huddle in fear before a mighty sea, and they cry out to Moses that it would have been better to remain as slaves than die in the desert. Moses's answer both assures and terrifies them, as he shouts out what God is about to do:

> Do not be afraid. Stand firm and you will see the deliverance the LORD will bring you today. The Egyptians you see today you will never see again. The LORD will fight for you; you need only to be still.
>
> Exodus 14:13–14

Being still was all they *could* do; they were closed in by the Red Sea in front of them and Egyptian chariots behind them. But it was in that place they witnessed something so colossal; God was flaunting His feathers in a way that would etch His faithfulness in their hearts. As the sea split in two before their eyes, they were invited not just to be spectators but to be participants in the miracle. The experience of walking through walls of water made them see, feel, touch, smell, and live what God did on their behalf. They could never forget this day—with a visceral experience so astonishing, so awe inspiring, they would never again doubt God's presence and His care for them. This was a miracle of miracles, and all they could do was be grateful they were there.

On the fifteenth day of the second month of their deliverance, Genesis 16 opens with the dialogue of these same Israelites. Forty-five days after witnessing the Red Sea part, this is the memory that was currently occupying their minds and hearts:

> If only we had died by the LORD's hand in Egypt! There we sat around pots of meat and ate all the food we wanted, but you have brought us out into this desert to starve this entire assembly to death.
>
> Exodus 16:3

Wait. What?

A month and a half after walking through a sea God parted for their freedom, *this* is the memory these people recount?

To be fair, these people were thirsty and hungry, and that never combines well for attitudes. However, there is something here to learn about the way we hold our memories—and how *what* we remember can either feed or starve our faith. Of all the memories for the Israelites to shout out, it seems particularly poignant that they would choose one they likely mustered from the ashes and embellished. To remember what they ate between hauling bricks and bearing beatings in Egypt seems like a bit of a reach, especially when their memory more recently held a massive miracle of God parting a sea. Maybe it's just me, but sitting around "pots of meat" also seems pretty unlikely in the midst of slavery. Though the Egyptians undoubtedly fed them so they could be strengthened for their workload, the taxing life they endured was hardly worth the few seconds of pleasure a meal may have brought. The insight this passage gives us is that it's not just the act of remembering—but *what* we remember—that builds or diminishes our faith.

> When we don't find a way to recount and remember what God has done, our minds are left to rewrite our memories with the doubt or fear we might be currently facing.

When we don't find a way to recount and remember what God has done, our minds are left to rewrite our memories with the doubt or fear we might be currently facing. Our fear has the power to filter what actually happened and can prevent us from gaining faith from what God did in the past. If we don't hold the hope of our stories, our memory can be reshaped by the stress and worry of our current circumstances. Studies of the brain show that our past is not set in stone; the way we remember it is impacted by what we are presently feeling. The neurons that access our memories of the past are controlled by brain activity that is happening now, so our present anxiety has the power to rewrite our memories—and even create an altered past. This is why it is so important to write, sing, draw, memorize, and repeat the details of our experience, so we can remind ourselves of God's faithfulness in what has happened to us. Then we can go back and find God's faithfulness again—in a way that our current stress and worry might not allow us to see.

Just one chapter before (in Exodus 15), the beautiful song that Miriam and Moses sang to celebrate their escape is recorded. But something happened between that song and the desert, because it's clear the people are no longer singing about what happened to them to reinforce their faith. Instead, the Israelites are worried about how God will provide for them, and their current circumstances cause them to develop spiritual amnesia. Their month-and-a-half-ago miracle is no longer sustaining their belief. By the end of Exodus 15, the song of victory that began the chapter has already started to be replaced by grumbling (see v. 24). By the beginning of Exodus 16, their grumbling has gone full tilt, and instead of singing about God's faithfulness, their words to Moses are filled with fears and complaints. What we repeat we grow to believe, and if we fill our minds with all the bad things that might happen, we crowd out our confidence in how God will provide for us. Miriam's song of what God did for them needed to be sung not once, but daily, in order to set their future course.

Watch God's response: after the Israelites talk about sitting around eating pots of meat in Egypt, God decides they need a lesson to help their memory. Apparently, a sea parting wasn't enough to sustain their faith for more than a month, so in Exodus 16:4, God instructs Moses about the daily faith lesson He is going to provide:

> I will rain down bread from heaven for you. The people are to go out each day and gather enough for that day. In this way I will test them and see whether they will follow my instructions.

As you read on, the miracle of daily manna was not a one-time occurrence—it was a forty-year daily experience (Exodus 16:35). Admittedly the repetition probably led them to crave a little variety, but notice how God did this repetitive miracle following the Israelites' amnesia after seeing God's power displayed. It seems the Lord wanted to drum the lesson of His faithfulness into their very bones, so every day for forty years they were going to experience it. If they couldn't hold their memory of the parting of a sea, God would make sure the manna miracle would be something they'd not be able to forget. God's faithfulness was not going to be remembered in the largeness of His rescue this time; instead, God taught the Israelites to trust Him through the repetitiveness of His provision. In the years of being fed daily, they grew to depend on God to provide for them, which is how God grows our faith.

But, if they hadn't lived day-to-day with a need, they couldn't have experienced this miracle. Exodus 16:19–20 says they were not able to save what they had until the next day; they were forced to depend daily on what God would provide. When the Israelites saw manna appear every morning, they eventually moved from wondering whether it would come to expecting it to happen. They learned they could anticipate God's faithfulness, so they were freer to let go and trust—because they knew by experience God would come through. This lesson also taught them they had to open their hands to the way God would choose to provide for them. Manna literally meant "What is it?" Every time they ate it, they reestablished God as the creator and provider of their food.

God trained the Israelites to depend on His faithfulness by becoming the daily source of their provision. When God wants to grow our faith, our life is vacated of what we ourselves can provide. The process is not comfortable, but this experience pushes us to feel our dependence. Whether we face a diagnosis, a job termination, or a catastrophic loss, these experiences viscerally show us what God alone is able to provide. It is in that place of need that we are desperate enough to reach out for what is clearly beyond us. In the desert—with no food, water, or way to provide for themselves—the Israelites saw, touched, and tasted the faithfulness of God.

This experience was not just lived; God wanted to make sure this time it would be remembered. It seems that God wanted to guide the Israelites into their future knowing that no matter what they faced, they could hold on to their faith. Here's what Moses says to them:

> This is what the LORD has commanded: "Take an omer of manna and keep it for the generations to come, so they can see the bread I gave you to eat in the wilderness when I brought you out of Egypt."
>
> Exodus 16:32

The Israelites are instructed to keep a portion of God's provision so they can return to it to remember God's faithfulness. Because the manna disappeared and reappeared daily, Aaron was instructed to put some in a jar and keep it before the Lord for generations to come. Perhaps this is a word for us as well, to write down, draw, build, collect, or keep something in a box to remind ourselves of the times we've experienced God's provision. Keeping a tangible reminder of God's faithfulness will hold it firmly in our memory so it can encourage us for what's to come.

The next chapter reveals that God continues to have the Israelites write memories on scrolls and build altars when they experience God's faithfulness (see Exodus 17:14–15). It's apparent one manna lesson is not enough; God knows we need weekly (if not daily) reminders to move forward in our faith.

Repetitive remembering helps forgetful people know that even if we can't predict what God will bring, we know God will be faithful. The lesson of manna is a relevant lesson for us all.

LUKE 24: Answers Are Revealed by Looking Back

When Luke 24 opens, Jesus is dead, and many of His followers' hopes for who He would be have died with Him. They were questioning why they had spent the last three years following Him—leaving jobs, families, friends, and most (if not all) of what had previously filled their lives. It had only been two days since Jesus's crucifixion, so most of them were either locked up in fear or had dispersed from where they were following Him. They didn't want to be recognized for believing what now appeared to be a lie.

Luke 24:13 begins with two of them walking to a village called Emmaus, seven miles from Jerusalem. Verse 14 says, "They were talking with each other about everything that had happened," so they were likely recounting their experience with Jesus and wondering where they went wrong. The passage lists only one of them by name, Cleopas (v. 18), which is a reminder that Jesus had other devoted followers along with His twelve disciples. As Cleopas and the other traveler talked and walked, the passage says the resurrected Jesus joined them, but "they were kept from recognizing him" (v. 16), so He must have looked different from when He was alive. In their conversation, we learn how God infuses our memory with new insights to strengthen our faith.

Jesus joins their conversation disguised as a fellow traveler and asks them what they are discussing (v. 17). It's clear He wants them to recount their conversation, and since the passage mentions their faces are downcast, it seems Jesus wants to take them back to revive their faith. They assume Jesus is a foreigner, otherwise He would know the events that had just transpired. Jesus didn't just know the events, He *was* the event, but He wants to hear how these two followers would recount their experience of who He was.

The two tell this "stranger" all about Jesus, and how they were taken in by how powerful He was "in word and deed before God and all the people" (v. 19). It's interesting that before Jesus speaks to them, He wants to hear what they remember about who He was. Their memory was where Jesus looked first to find their faith.

The followers talk about all the events they saw—and how they witnessed Jesus being handed over and crucified. Then they share the words that the disguised Jesus was undoubtedly waiting to hear: "We had hoped that he was the one who was going to redeem Israel" (v. 21).

Before Jesus responds, they tell Him that it had been three days since this all happened. Some of the women were talking about the tomb being empty, and a couple of their companions had gone to the tomb themselves and confirmed the report. The two stop right there—just short of affirming the possibility of Jesus's resurrection. Their faith couldn't stretch to believe the possibility that Jesus might actually be alive.

That's when Jesus speaks up—and He must have initially surprised them when He chided them for not believing what the prophets had spoken. When He showed them what the Scriptures said about how the Christ would have to suffer and die before entering His glory, they were silenced; it's clear by the way they urged Him to stay that they were drawn to what He shared. Still unaware that it is Jesus who is with them, they invite the mysterious stranger to stay and share a meal with them. When Jesus breaks the bread, "their eyes were opened and they recognized him, and he disappeared from their sight" (Luke 24:31).

This passage is the first time Jesus speaks to people who can't see who He is and then leads them to have faith in Him. It will be the first of many times to come. From this point forward, all people will come to faith believing in an unseen Messiah. This passage records the first time the post-resurrected Christ drew people to Himself.

We also discover once more that what we remember shapes our faith—but this story reveals how our memory can give us new insights that deepen our understanding. Jesus begins by asking these followers what they remember, then takes them to the Scriptures to fill in what they didn't know. Their faith grew by going back to Scriptures they had already read—and seeing prophecies that were written but that couldn't be fulfilled until Jesus was here on earth to live them. By going back to those Scriptures, they could understand the mystery of what was transpiring after His death.

We can't miss that it was when Jesus broke the bread that the followers' eyes were opened and they recognized Him (Luke 24:30–31). This scene could be considered the first post-crucifixion communion, because these two had the first experience of breaking bread to recognize Jesus in their midst. He had been with them all along on their journey, but now they could see Him. This experience brought Him into their presence in a way they had previously missed.

When Jesus breaks the bread and their eyes are opened, we are reminded of Him saying "Here is my body" in the upper room with His disciples. Jesus reveals that the practice of breaking bread to experience His presence will continue, and these two followers experience it first. Today, we continue this practice all over the world in churches and gatherings. When we remember Jesus's death and resurrection through communion, we are celebrating the most important memory to hold about our faith: Jesus is alive!

This passage in Luke 24 reinforces what we learned in the two previous passages: remembering is God's way of equipping us with faith to face our future. After these two followers looked back with Jesus on the road to Emmaus, their faith was strengthened enough to return and tell the others, so they all could move forward in their belief.

Now they could face the uncertainty of what might happen to them with new confidence, and going back to Jerusalem was proof of their new boldness. No longer were they cowering from being recognized as believers; they joined the others to recount their stories so they could spread their resurrection faith.

> Sometimes by recounting what happened to us in the past, new insights can inform our memory of the experience.

A last observation in this passage is what happened to the two followers after Jesus disappeared, just as they finally recognized Him. The first thing they did was turn to each other to discuss what they had just experienced, presumably to solidify what they had seen.

Luke 24:32 reads, "They asked each other, 'Were not our hearts burning within us while he talked with us on the road and opened the Scriptures to us?'"

Just as Jesus pointed the two believers to Scriptures that they had previously misunderstood, now these two looked back over their conversation on the road with Jesus. Looking back not only allowed them to solidify what they remembered but to identify feelings that they had previously overlooked or missed. Sometimes by recounting what happened to us in the past, new insights can inform our memory of the experience. After recognizing that it was Jesus who was with them all the time, these two were able to go back to their memory of what happened and recall what they previously missed.

Their response in verse 33 shows how their faith was strengthened. Instead of continuing to run away from being recognized, now they had new courage to return to Jerusalem. Once in Jerusalem, they found the others, and verses 34–35 say they all shared testimonies to strengthen each other's faith. These two followers could now help strengthen the faith of others with what they had experienced for themselves.

Each of these three stories reveals different insights on how to be strengthened spiritually from the past: go back to where you've seen God work—remember the right things—and let God infuse your memory with new insights. The strength you get from God's faithfulness in the past can embolden your future faith. Each of these passages shows us a different angle on what remembering can do for us when we are fearful about what might be coming. We grow stronger in our ability to live by faith when we make it a regular practice to look back.

REFLECTION QUESTIONS

1. As you read what God says to Jacob in Genesis 35:1, where do you think God would tell you to go back to in order to strengthen your faith? Is there a place in your life where God seems especially present? Where do you go for spiritual encouragement?

2. After reading about the Israelites in Exodus 16, what lessons do we learn about memory and faith? How do you remember what God has done for you? What could you do to hold on to your memories of how God has worked in your life?

3. Looking at Luke 24:32 and what the disciples say to each other after Jesus leaves them, have you ever discovered something by looking back that you couldn't see while it was happening? What does this encounter reveal about the way God meets us?

6

Holding On May Mean Letting Go

"JUST THROW YOURSELF BACK, and the ropes will hold you." My feet were facing him as he spoke; behind me there was nothing but a cliff. He had me tied in "on belay," but I couldn't feel the tension of the ropes around me. I would have to lean backward off the cliff to discover whether or not the ropes would hold.

"Um, this feels really wrong," I murmured, and when he didn't flinch, I reluctantly positioned myself for this disparity. I kept trying to test the rope by taking a small step back, but he made it clear it was an all-or-nothing choice. "You have to trust the rope, even if it doesn't feel like it will hold you," he said. "The more you trust, the easier it will be to let go."

His words suddenly reached beyond my current experience and entered my heart with a hint of recognition. That rope felt a lot like God.

In the moments before I leaned back over that cliff, it struck me how many hundreds of times I've felt like God was absent. As time revealed how God was holding me, the only thing that was actually absent was my trust. We only truly know whether or not God is holding us when the thing we are relying on is removed, and that's the part none of us wants to experience. But it's in that chasm of full dependence where God builds our trust.

What's interesting about rappelling is that the only way to mess things up is when you *don't* trust that the rope will hold you. If you try to "help" the rope by keeping your body forward, you actually take away from what the rope is meant to do. (I tried it, and it wasn't pretty.) In a very real sense, you have to let go in order to hold on—something that is true in relationships, and especially true in our spiritual life. While holding on and letting go seem like opposites, when it comes to faith, they are two halves of the same truth.

> The more we let go and trust, the more we experience being held by God.

In our relationship with God, we are called repeatedly to let go of what we think we need, or might be too tightly holding. Oddly, the more we let go and trust, the more we experience being held by God. Letting go can feel like death, especially when what we think we need to survive is taken from us. It is the removal of that thing we think we need that reveals in us the need to lean on God.

The next three stories show that whether you have to let go of your security, expectations about the way God shows up, or the life that should have been yours, God is there to hold you. You experience that truth not only in what happens next, but in who you become. The space between letting go and experiencing God's faithfulness is like being on a cliff, where fear and trust battle for your allegiance. What happens to your faith is dependent on which of them wins.

GENESIS 33: You Have to Let Go to Embrace What's Yours

His future had been stolen from him by his younger brother. Worse yet, his own mother was told this would happen, and she was an accomplice in the crime. The two of them had created a plan to trick his father into giving his blessing to his brother, Jacob. Now, years after missing the life that was supposed to be his, Esau has his chance to pay Jacob back.

To understand the power of what happens next in this passage, we need to go back to the beginning of Esau's story. Because he was the elder twin son of Isaac and Rebekah, the firstborn birthright was supposed to be his. However, before the twins were born, Rebekah was told by God that the older son would end up serving the younger. The story of Esau and Jacob begins with these words that Rebekah heard: "The LORD said to her, 'Two nations are in your womb, and two peoples from within you will be separated; one people will be stronger than the other, and the older will serve the younger'" (Genesis 25:23).

Here we see the mystery of God's foreknowledge, as God knew in advance what would happen with Jacob and Esau. But Rebekah decides to help God make this prophecy happen—much like her mother-in-law, Sarah, tried to do before (see Genesis 16:1–2). The line between what God foretold and what Jacob and Rebekah decide to do is where predestination and human choice come together in Esau's story. Between God's will, his mother's favoritism, and his brother's deception, it seems that Esau is mostly the victim in what became of his fate.

Jacob manipulated Esau twice—first by taunting him into trading his birthright for a meal, then by putting animal hair on his arms and face to disguise himself so his nearly blind father would bless him. It's a tragic scene when Esau comes back from hunting game for his father, ready to receive that blessing, and discovers he is too late:

> His father Isaac asked him, "Who are you?"
>
> "I am your son," he answered, "your firstborn, Esau."
>
> Isaac trembled violently and said, "Who was it, then, that hunted game and brought it to me? I ate it just before you came and I blessed him—and indeed he will be blessed!"
>
> When Esau heard his father's words, he burst out with a loud and bitter cry and said to his father, "Bless me—me too, my father!"
>
> But he said, "Your brother came deceitfully and took your blessing."
>
> Genesis 27:32–35

How do you accept your fate when you are the victim of someone else taking what belongs to you? The truth is, this happens every day—to people who are fired and replaced for unknown reasons, retirement funds that are lost in money-making schemes, spouses who are left after an affair. It's one thing to be a victim of circumstances gone bad; it's another thing when someone has made those circumstances happen. When someone else has stolen what should be yours, Esau's quiet, mostly unrecorded life is the one to watch.

Initially, the deception leaves Esau furious, and he plans to wait for his father to die and then kill Jacob (Genesis 27:41). But something changes in Esau; when we meet him years later in Genesis 33, he is a different man. In the silence of Esau's story between Genesis 27 and 33, the only verses that speak of him are when he tries to please his parents by marrying

Ishmael's daughter (Genesis 28:8–9). After all that happened to him in his family, this action reveals a seed of tenderness and vulnerability that is still present in Esau's heart. Five chapters and many years of life later, it's clear Esau has let go of what should have been his, allowing the seed of tenderness, rather than his justified resentment, to grow.

When Esau is first mentioned in Genesis 33, he is coming with four hundred men toward Jacob (v. 1). Jacob sends an entourage of people before him, and as Esau approaches him, he bows down to the ground seven times (vv. 2–3). He is met by surprise when Esau runs to him and embraces him. When Esau throws his arms around Jacob's neck and kisses him, they both weep, and the years of deception and bitterness between them instantly melt in the force of Esau's grace.

Esau confirms this force at work by his words to Jacob:

> "What's the meaning of all these flocks and herds I met?"
> "To find favor in your eyes, my lord," [Jacob] said.
> But Esau said, "I already have plenty, my brother. Keep what you have for yourself."
>
> Genesis 33:8–9

"I already have plenty" indicates that Esau has a reservoir of God's grace that God has instilled in him. We can only assume in the silence of the chapters that follow Jacob's story that, somewhere along the way, Esau let go of the life he once wanted and fully embraced the life he had. One would expect with all he had to let go of that Esau would be filled with resentment; he had been forced to live a second-rate life without the blessing he wanted. Instead, it appears that Esau took the blessing he was given and made the best of the life he had. And along the way, forgiveness came and took his bitterness, leaving him with an unencumbered heart.

It seems that even though Jacob got the birthright, Esau's character confirms his place as the older, wiser brother. Jacob is so moved by Esau's grace that he begs him to receive his gifts:

> "If I have found favor in your eyes, accept this gift from me. For to see your face is like seeing the face of God, now that you have received me favorably. Please accept the present that was brought to you, for God has been gracious to me and I have all I need." And because Jacob insisted, Esau accepted it.
>
> Genesis 33:10–11

"To see your face is like seeing the face of God" shows what happens to others when we allow grace to lead us. This is no easy task when people have taken something from us that should have been ours. In his book *Forgive and Forget*, Lewis B. Smedes says when you forgive someone, "you set a prisoner free,"[1] which is a perfect image of what happens when we absolve someone of our resentment. But the surprise comes with the last part of Smedes's definition: "you discover that the real prisoner was yourself."[2] This is the part of forgiveness that Esau embodies with his life. Esau had been freed from the bitterness that could have kept him locked down, estranged, and alienated. The four hundred people with Esau when he meets Jacob reveal that Esau has multiplied his assets and led a full and prosperous life. It may not have been the life he thought he deserved, but it was the life that God had given to him. Instead of living in resentment for what he should have gotten, Esau clearly made the best of what he had. When he tells Jacob in verse 9 that he doesn't need his gifts because

1. Lewis B. Smedes, *Forgive and Forget* (New York: Harper and Row, 1987), 133.
2. Smedes, *Forgive and Forget*, 133.

he already has plenty, he shows that he is fulfilled and satisfied. By letting go of his resentment about the life that should have been his, Esau found he was held by God. And his face reflected it.

Many scholars believe the story of Jacob and Esau's reunion is a parallel and forerunner of the parable Jesus tells of the prodigal. In the book *Jacob and the Prodigal*, author Kenneth E. Bailey reveals many similarities between the two stories and observes it's highly possible that when Jesus told the parable in Luke 15, he had this story in mind.[3] If this premise is true, Jesus must have taken Esau's example—running to Jacob with his grace—and used it to illustrate the extravagant love of the Father. To imagine that, years after Esau was gone, a hint of his life would be found in Jesus's parable about God's love reveals what God can do when we let go of our lives.

Esau may have lost his birthright, but he certainly won with the way he lived his life.

1 KINGS 19: You Need to Leave Room for How God Shows Up

In *Prince Caspian*, one of the books in the CHRONICLES OF NARNIA series, there is a scene between Aslan and Lucy that gives us a clue about the unpredictability of God's presence. For those of you not familiar with C. S. Lewis's CHRONICLES OF NARNIA (please get them immediately), Aslan is the Christ figure in all seven books. When Lucy and the other children had last encountered Aslan, they experienced him coming in power to save them. So when Lucy sees him quietly shadowing her after they had called on his power again, she is startled by his calm. Aslan

3. Kenneth E. Bailey, *Jacob and the Prodigal: How Jesus Retold Israel's Story* (Downers Grove, IL: IVP, 2003) 216–18.

gently informs her that this time, he will not be fighting the battle for them. Instead, she will be fighting it herself. This is her response:

> "Oh dear, oh dear, and I was so pleased at finding you again. And I thought you'd let me stay. And I thought you'd come roaring in and frighten all the enemies away, like last time. And now everything is going to be horrid."[4]

The Aslan who comes to Lucy this time acts in a new and different way than last time. In Aslan's response to Lucy, we get an important insight about God:

> "It is hard for you, little one. . . . But things never happen the same way twice."[5]

Letting go takes many forms, and one of them is our expectation of who God will be for us. When you experience God a certain way, you might expect that God will come that way again. But God's presence is notoriously unpredictable, which is both frustrating and exhilarating. It's what holds us dependent, and keeps us watching and waiting for the new way God will show up.

There is no Old Testament figure who learned this lesson more than the prophet Elijah. As one of the most powerful prophets in Israel's history, he stands alone with Moses in the miracles he watched God do. When Elijah is introduced in 1 Kings 17, he spends time being fed miraculously by ravens in a ravine, then moves from there to participate in a boy's resurrection (see v. 6–22). For his crowning story of faith, he

---

4. C. S. Lewis, *Prince Caspian: The Return to Narnia* (New York: HarperCollins, 2002), 150.

5. Lewis, *Prince Caspian*, 150.

challenges four hundred and fifty prophets of Baal in a competition and watches one of God's most dramatic victories take place (see 1 Kings 18). Yet after all these miraculous displays of God's power, Elijah is chased by one angry queen, and he runs away to brood alone under a broom tree, exhausted and depressed. Here's his prayer: "I have had enough, Lord. . . . Take my life; I am no better than my ancestors" (1 Kings 19:4).

Have you ever been there? Elijah is where so many of us are after a long day of ministry, when people are unhappy, critical, or seemingly out to get us. Despite how we may have just witnessed God's power, now we want to throw in the towel and give up. This is one of the most tender scenes in the Old Testament because of the way God meets Elijah in his depression. God sends an angel to feed and strengthen him, and doesn't even begin to speak to him until he takes two long naps. Once Elijah is rested and strengthened, he is able to go to Horeb and find a cave to sleep in, safely hidden from his enemy. And after he wakes up, we see the same lesson Lucy learned about Aslan in what Elijah learns about God.

> The word of the Lord came to him: "What are you doing here, Elijah?"
>
> He replied, "I have been very zealous for the Lord God Almighty. The Israelites have rejected your covenant, torn down your altars, and put your prophets to death with the sword. I am the only one left, and now they are trying to kill me too."
>
> The Lord said, "Go out and stand on the mountain in the presence of the Lord, for the Lord is about to pass by."
>
> 1 Kings 19:9–11

In verses 11–13, Elijah is invited to come out to the mouth of the cave, and God sends a powerful wind, shattering the mountains. But the Lord is not in the wind. After the wind, there is an earthquake, but the Lord is not in the earthquake. After the earthquake, there is a fire, but the Lord is not in the fire. Then finally, after the fire, there is a gentle whisper, and when Elijah hears it, he pulls his cloak over his face.

God meets Elijah in a whisper. After Elijah watched God control the ravens to feed him, raise a boy from the dead, and rain fire down from heaven to prove His majesty, he is now invited to converse with God in a still small voice. As it turns out, this manifestation of God is just what Elijah needs.

Lucy learns a similar lesson as Elijah does in this passage. After crying out in disappointment that Aslan was not going to fight the battle for her, Aslan welcomes Lucy to bury her small head in his mane. And in their quiet huddle, something miraculous happens. She feels Aslan's lion strength growing within her, and she emerges from his mane with these words:

"I'm sorry, Aslan," she said. "I'm ready now."

"Now you are a lioness," said Aslan. "And now all Narnia will be renewed."[6]

Lucy had longed for the old Aslan who came and fought the battle while she watched him. This time Aslan wants to watch *her* fight the battle with his strength. It wouldn't be as easy, but it would grow Lucy in the way Aslan wanted her faith to develop. She would learn how to access Aslan's strength within her, and she would grow in her confidence for what she could do.

There is one more difference in Aslan that Lucy notices when she sees him in this encounter. In their conversation, we get another insight about how God grows our faith.

6. Lewis, *Prince Caspian*, 148.

106

"Aslan," said Lucy, "you're bigger."

"That's because you are older, little one," answered he.

"Not because you are?"

"I am not. But every year you grow, you will find me bigger."[7]

In this brief exchange, C. S. Lewis brilliantly describes what it's like to experience God in different forms and to grow in our spiritual understanding. The more mature we become, the bigger God is. We don't grow in our ability to explain God, we grow in our ability to trust Him. The more we experience God's mysterious faithfulness, the more we are able to wait in trust for how God will show up.

> We don't grow in our ability to explain God, we grow in our ability to trust Him.

Elijah is standing at the mouth of the cave when God meets him in a whisper. God asks Elijah the same question as before, inviting Elijah to pour his feelings out again before God gives him a response.

> Then a voice said to him, "What are you doing here, Elijah?"
>
> He replied, "I have been very zealous for the Lord God Almighty. The Israelites have rejected your covenant, torn down your altars, and put your prophets to death with the sword. I am the only one left, and now they are trying to kill me too."
>
> The Lord said to him, "Go back the way you came, and go to the Desert of Damascus. When you get there, anoint Hazael king over Aram. Also, anoint Jehu son of Nimshi king over Israel, and anoint Elisha son of Shaphat from Abel Meholah to succeed you as prophet."
>
> 1 Kings 19:13–16

7. Lewis, *Prince Caspian*, 148.

God's response is to send Elijah back to the life he had left with an assurance of God's presence—even if he doesn't always feel it. Elijah now knows that the presence of God takes many forms, and the form isn't always (or ever) the way we expect. We may have to let go of how we experienced God before to be open to a new way of discovering Him. Instead of assuming God's absence because He's not coming the way He did previously, we stand ready to see God in a new way.

God may come in power and might, or we might experience God in quietness and subtlety. God may take our battle and fight it alone, or invite us to fight it with His help. We may not be able to predict the way God comes, but we can live expectantly that it will happen. As long as we let go of our stipulation for how it will be, we can be there to witness it when God shows up. That's the lesson of Elijah's life.

JOHN 2: You May Have to Act before You See

They are remembered as nameless servants at a wedding, but they were the witnesses of Jesus's first miracle. Others saw and tasted the result of this miracle; only these servants saw how it was done. I like to put myself in their place and imagine what it must have been like to step out and do what this teacher had commanded. Undoubtedly, they saw their livelihoods flash before their eyes—knowing they might be humiliated, ridiculed, or possibly even kicked out on the streets.

From the text, we aren't given any information about how these servants felt when Jesus asked them to fill the six stone water jars with water. John 2:6 says each jar held twenty to thirty gallons, and the only thing we are told is that these dear servants filled the jars "to the brim" (v. 7). When Jesus tells them to draw some out and take it to the master of the banquet, I can only imagine the terror that must have bubbled up inside them. Jesus had performed zero miracles at this point, but He must have carried some authority for the servants to trust Him enough to obey this crazy command. With three words, we discover what the servants did next: "They did so" (v. 8).

No argument or word of hesitation. What they might have felt inside is a matter we will never know. All we know is what the passage says next: "The master of the banquet tasted the water that had been turned into wine. He did not realize where it had come from, though the servants who had drawn the water knew" (v. 9).

For a moment, the servants must have nervously looked at each other, wondering what on earth the master of the banquet would say or do to them. What they probably least expected was this response:

> Then he called the bridegroom aside and said, "Everyone brings out the choice wine first and then the cheaper wine after the guests have had too much to drink; but you have saved the best till now."
>
> John 2:9–10

By sticking their necks out, these servants got front-row seats to Jesus's first miracle. But they had to let go of what might have happened to them in order to experience what no one else did. Verse 9 emphasizes that the servants who drew the water were the only ones who knew where this delicious wine had originated. What they discovered about Jesus was more—and bigger—than anyone else could see, because they were firsthand witnesses of what took place.

This surprise miracle in John 2 carries the insight that when we step out in faith, we become firsthand witnesses to God's power and glory. The wedding guests got to taste the wine, but only the servants who risked their livelihood saw how the wine was made. They had to trust that Jesus knew what He was talking about when He made the preposterous request to fill the stone water jugs and then serve some to the master at the banquet. Because Jesus had no miracles in His résumé, they only had the words of Jesus's mother—who told them ahead of time to do whatever He said (v. 5).

I imagine that some of them may have thought she was a little biased as His mother—especially after Jesus gave them the strange instructions. They saw that Jesus had followers, so they knew He was a compelling teacher, but they had no point of reference for what He could actually do. Mary and Jesus were *not* the servants' masters, yet somehow the servants had enough faith to put their lives on the line and *do* what they asked of them. After the servants realized what they poured into the master's glass, they must have looked at each other in wonder over what they alone knew.

One other detail to note in this story is the extent of the servants' obedience in their response to Jesus. I don't know about you, but if I were instructed to fill stone jars with water—when the need was wine—I probably would not have filled them to the brim. At twenty or thirty gallons apiece, filling those stone jars to the brim seems a response of courageous obedience. Especially since the request to fill the jars was not given by the host but by one of the guests, who they barely knew.

The servants may have observed Jesus with His disciples at the wedding and maybe even had heard stories about Him. Somehow they saw something that compelled them to obedience—either because of how others were drawn to Him or because He spoke with an authority that they decided to trust. Still, these servants took a great risk, and in doing so they got to see a fuller picture of who Jesus was than others who had been around Him. Jesus invited these servants into

His very first miracle, and they not only witnessed it, they participated in it—and they were even able to hear the compliments for what they didn't do.

The servants not only saw Jesus do this miracle, they watched Him step aside and not publicly take credit for it. This must have made an impression on them too. Undoubtedly, the wedding host (presumably their boss) received praise for wine he neither produced nor purchased. These servants allowed the wedding host to save face in front of the guests because they were willing to trust what Jesus told them to do. They got to witness and usher forth a part of Jesus no one had seen yet, and the space between filling the jars with water—and the master's response—is where Jesus grew their faith.

I like to imagine how the servants felt when the master of the banquet not only liked the wine but called it the best wine of the evening. Those servants could have been blamed for the bridegroom's humiliation; instead, they were responsible for this incredible praise because they took this risk. Jars of water had not just turned into jugs of wine, they held the finest wine of the evening, and these servants were the only ones brought in close enough to see it. In the abundant grace delivered with unpretentiousness, the servants saw a glimpse of what Jesus continued to do throughout His life.

This story affirms that when we are willing to let go and risk what *might* happen, our faith grows when we see what *does* happen. However, it's no easy task to hang in the unknowing space between *might* and *does*. In some ways, it's similar to standing with your back to the edge of a mountain, with a loose rope around your waist, and being instructed to lean back over the cliff so the rope can hold you. What you feel, and what you do, carry two different possibilities—and the good news is, you don't have to feel completely confident when you decide. The less there is of you, the more there can be of God.

Faith fills in where our confidence lacks, and God grows bigger with each insecure opportunity we are willing to give Him. We will never know what these servants at the wedding felt, but we can assume this event changed them for life. And we can't dismiss what it took to put their livelihoods on the line, not knowing what would happen to them. Letting go is part of holding on to what we believe God will do when we step out in faith.

The less there is of you, the more there can be of God.

In each of these three stories we discover that holding on and letting go are two sides of living by faith; we have to let go to see what God can do or be for us. Esau discovered a reservoir of grace in his acceptance of what happened to him, Elijah discovered the many forms God takes, and the servants became the audience of the first recorded miracle of Jesus's life. By letting go of what they had, knew, or felt, each of these people experienced God filling in the gaps for them. Their hold on God grew as they let go of themselves.

If we don't give God space to fill our inadequacies, it's likely that our experience of God will be benign and distant. God doesn't push into our lives past our invitation; we have to let God be something bigger for us in order to see something bigger of God. If we are committed to holding our own, we'll never experience what it means to hold on to Him. The space where our sufficiency ends is where God loves most to show up.

REFLECTION QUESTIONS

1. When you read about Esau in Genesis 33, is there anything you learned about him that you didn't know?

How does his forgiveness of Jacob speak to your relationships? Is there anything from the past that you need to let go of to experience more freedom in your heart?

2. What does 1 Kings 19 reveal about God in the way He met Elijah? Has God ever met you tenderly in your discouragement? Have you ever had to let go of your preconceived notions to learn something new about God?

3. Look at John 2:1–11. What stands out to you most in this story? Have you ever had to step out in faith and do something when you weren't sure about the outcome? What is your next step in trusting God enough to partner with Him?

7

God Is in the Hard

I HAD ROLLED OUT OF THE BED onto the floor with no strength to face the life in front of me. I wanted to erase the words plastered in my memory, after a brief waking hope that it had all been a dream. Sleep had offered me a gentle escape, but the morning reintroduced me to my reality. My year-and-a-half engagement had ended, and in three days, I was getting on a plane to be the keynote speaker at a conference, where I was supposed to give a message about the love of God.

"How can I speak of your love when I feel totally abandoned?" I whispered into the air, picturing my words bouncing off the specks on my ceiling. My next question was scarier. "Is this what it comes to—telling others what I am no longer experiencing myself?"

I waited in the silence to see if there was any answer. I couldn't imagine surviving the day, let alone leaving behind a never-to-be-used wedding dress and piles of no-longer-relevant shower gifts—and heading to a conference where I was scheduled to bring hope. After what seemed to be several hours, I tried shouting to the air again, bolstered by the apparent lack of interest from the silent God I was trying to address.

"How could you let this happen?" I whimpered. "My engagement made me a poster child for people waiting for the right one, and this is the twisted end you write?"

The humiliation of the previous night's breakup—after my fiancé returned from his nine-month deployment—was the chapter of life I was carrying to the conference. I knew something was going wrong about halfway through his time away, but he wanted to wait to talk about it until he got home. I had been counseled by a chaplain to wait and see what would happen, so my life had been left in limbo. For three months, I wasn't sure if I was still engaged or not, and during the previous evening's dinner date, I found out I was not.

"How can I convince people to follow you if this is the way you've handled my life?"

Then it happened—penetrating the silence, a voice spoke to me that wasn't me. I'm not sure if I heard or felt it, but I still remember the words clear as day.

Don't you worry about me, little girl, the Voice said, low and deep, and for a moment, I stopped breathing.

Just tell your story, the Voice continued, and then the moment was gone.

I wrote the words I heard in my journal, and somewhere in a tucked-away box, I still have it. What ended up happening at the conference is that I discovered something new about God.

The number of people who responded to the rawness of my unfinished (and I thought pretty depressing) testimony made it clear that when God calls you to hardship, you don't carry it without Him. And if you take the risk to expose your pain before it is resolved, it has the capacity to reach others

116

with a power that nothing else can touch. That weekend—and every time I spoke during this painful season—I experienced the presence of God.

I believe we wait too long to give our testimonies. We think people need the happy ending of God's deliverance in order to be drawn to faith. But God speaks most poignantly through people hanging on to Him in the midst of hardship. Probably because in the midst of the hardship is where most people live.

Hardship changes you or breaks you, but it probably won't evade you. In the midst of it we discover that hardship is not a sign of God's absence; it is where God's greatest power dwells. The fol-

> Hardship is not a sign of God's absence; it is where God's greatest power dwells.

lowing stories show how three different people in Scripture responded to their call to hardship, and what they learned about God.

GENESIS 16, 21: Sometimes We're Led Where We Don't Want to Go

"Go back to your mistress and submit to her," Hagar heard in the desert after she was rescued (Genesis 16:9). After fleeing from her suffering, she was told by the angel who found her to return to her hard life.

It seems like a paradox—why would the Rescuer send Hagar back to circumstances that drove her to escape? *Unless* it was partly an inside rescue—one that wasn't designed to remove her from her circumstances but strengthen her to face them with God's help. Perhaps Hagar was rescued from the belief that she had to bear her pain alone.

When the angel finds Hagar in the desert, she has run away from Sarah and Abraham. They had used her as a surrogate mother for a baby that they had planned to take from her and raise. God had promised them a child, but they were desperate because no child seemed to be on the horizon. So they took God's promise—and used Hagar's body—to fulfill the promise themselves. Hagar did not hide her unhappiness over being used, so Sarah asks for Abraham's permission to punish her (Genesis 16:4). This is what drives Hagar to flee, and when God finds Hagar in the desert, she is afraid and alone.

The first words out of the angel's mouth reveal how intimately God knows her. He proclaims her name—along with the position she held—before asking her why she was there: "Hagar, servant of Sarai, where have you come from and where are you going?" (Genesis 16:8 ESV).

If the angel already knew so much about who she was, it seems obvious that he would know the answers to these questions. Yet he still invites Hagar to pour out her heart about what happened, and all that had brought her to this place.

"I'm running away from my mistress Sarai," (v. 8) she states, and the response she gets is stark and unexpected. The angel immediately tells her she needs to go back. But that's not all the angel says—he gives her a promise to take with her that must have given her a glimmer of hope: "I will increase your descendants so much that they will be too numerous to count" (v. 10).

The angel gives her a prophecy for a future with her unborn child. However, the road to that future is probably not what she had hoped. She has to go back to Abraham and Sarah, have her baby in their house, and trust that the Lord will protect her. But the next verse indicates that Hagar has the assurance that she doesn't return there alone. Hagar gives God a name—and her words reveal new insight about who God is in her life. "You are the God who sees me," (v. 13) she says, and from now on, she knows she is watched in all her circumstances. She may have to return to the place she wanted to leave, but she doesn't go there alone. The God who sees her will be by her side.

In Hagar's story, we can observe that God's presence is not measured by the ups and downs of our circumstances. God is with us, no matter what hardships we face. In this episode of Hagar's life, God comes alongside Hagar and calls her to "do hard" *with* Him. Scripture is silent about what Hagar felt when the angel told her to go back to Sarah, but we know by the name she gives God that she left with a new awareness that she was not alone.

"I have now seen the One who sees me," (v. 13) she says, and after proclaiming this, she returns to her mistress. The recognition of having God's attention gives her the perseverance she needs to see her story through. When she returns to Sarah and Abraham, she gives birth to Ishmael, and after a few years, Ishmael gets circumcised the same day as his father (Genesis 17:26). In the next few chapters, we hear no more about Hagar or Ishmael until Sarah gives birth to Isaac, and in chapter 21, Sarah tells Abraham she wants his "other family" sent away.

God had sustained Hagar through her remaining years of living as Sarah's mistress, but in chapter 21, it becomes clear that season has ended. Ironically, Hagar has grown comfortable in her security as a mistress and a mother, and when she is dismissed and dropped off in the middle of the desert, she is—once more—afraid and alone. After watching the last drop of water Abraham had given her disappear, Hagar leaves Ishmael under a bush because she doesn't want to see his suffering. God meets her again in the middle of her desperation, this time sending an angel to give her these words of comfort and hope: "What is the matter, Hagar? Do not be afraid; God has heard the boy crying as he lies there. Lift the boy up and take him by the hand, for I will make him into a great nation" (Genesis 21:17–18).

This time, the angel does not tell her to go back; instead he gives her a promise about the future. By proclaiming who Ishmael will become, God gives Hagar hope for what lies ahead. Hagar's provision won't come by being sent back to Abraham and Sarah; instead she is invited to move forward with the knowledge of who her son will become for her. He will grow into adulthood and become a great nation, so Hagar can rest in the provision he will give her in years to come.

Hagar is finally called to move on from serving a mistress who is jealous of her, but her freedom comes with fear and uncertainty. In chapter 16, she had run away, but this time she is sent away, so we can assume she had somehow gotten used to the limitations of her life. Sometimes we need to be pried from difficulty simply because it has become familiar to us. We become comfortable with something less than we deserve because we've gotten used to it, and we've accommodated ourselves to survive. What is ironic in Hagar's story is that when she ran away, God sent her back, but when she is sent away, God tells her to move forward. In different ways, both were rescues—but they were specifically catered to instill strengths in Hagar that she needed to develop in order to grow. God brings our rescues in packages that push us to face fears and insecurities that He wants us to overcome.

Genesis 21:19 says when God opened Hagar's eyes, she saw God's provision for her. Whether it was there before and she didn't see it, we don't know, but sometimes our suffering obstructs us from seeing God's help. God's immediate provision is a well of water (v. 19), but in verse 20, it's a promise of a future for Ishmael. The fact that verse 21 says that Hagar found Ishmael an Egyptian wife reveals that Hagar likely made her way back to her original home. Hagar was introduced as

Sarah's "Egyptian servant" (Genesis 16:1 ESV); now it appears she has gone back to the Egyptian community where she had once belonged.

Hagar is never mentioned again, but Ishmael is mentioned when he helps Isaac bury Abraham (see Genesis 25:9). Genesis 25:1–2 reveals that Abraham married someone else after Sarah died, and had six more children, but Abraham's burial highlights Ishmael's importance, because he and Isaac were the only ones there. In Genesis 28:8–9, we discover that Isaac's son Esau marries one of Ishmael's daughters to try to please Isaac. These incidental verses indicate that a closeness between Ishmael and Isaac must have continued throughout their lives.

Looking back on Hagar's journey, we wonder if one reason Hagar was called to return to Abraham and Sarah in chapter 16 was to solidify the relationship that would develop between Ishmael and Isaac. As time moves on, we are able to see that God not only accompanies us in the hard, He has a purpose for it that goes beyond our own lives. "The God who sees" us has a vision for our difficult seasons that often impacts more people than we can imagine. He takes our painful chapters and includes them in a story that only He could write.

JOB 2: God's Affirmation Isn't Measured by Circumstances

Job's wife speaks only two sentences, and her reputation as a miserable woman is sealed in the Old Testament. Yet digging deeper into the reasons behind her words, we can't help but wonder if we might have responded the same way ourselves. Her husband's suffering was her suffering—apart from the boils on his body, she experienced every one of his losses. Yet

Scripture is silent about her grief; all we are given in Job 2 is the brevity of her caustic response.

Because of what had happened to Job, she too lost everything. She was by default a victim of Satan's scheme to get Job to renounce his faith. For years she had witnessed her husband's integrity; his devotion to God was unrivaled by any of her friends' husbands. Yet it was clear to her that the God she had watched Job serve and love had abandoned him by allowing these crushing blows.

Like Job, she knew nothing about the bet between God and Satan. Unlike Job, she did not have the faith to separate their traumatic circumstances from God's love. As her husband sat among the ashes of what used to be their life, she gave him this gloomy advice: "Are you still maintaining your integrity? Curse God and die!" (Job 2:9).

These are the only sentences we hear from her, with no knowledge of the emotion or actions behind them. She sounds angry and caustic, yet imagining her words being delivered with a trembling voice, coming from a tear-stained face, we might find sympathy for the way she felt. Who of us hasn't been tempted to have these feelings about God after experiencing a catastrophic loss or being faced with a dire diagnosis? The first moments of our response to devastation might be a scene none of us would want others to see. Yet these words are all that are written about Job's wife, and unfortunately, they are words that have branded her life.

Job's wife had a faith that was defined by her circumstances. She had not matured past the place where suffering meant God's absence and prosperity was a sign of God's love. Job, on the other hand, saw his whole life in the hands of the God he worshiped. This is clear by his response to his wife's words: "You are talking like a foolish woman. Shall we accept good from God, and not trouble?" (Job 2:10).

Covered in boils, isolated, and distressed, Job feels no entitlement to comfort and prosperity. He has questions about why this suffering has happened to him, but he knows that the goodness of his life has been a gift—so he submits to the hard. As we saw in the first chapter of this book, this scene is merely the beginning of Job's journey. Job will question, probe, challenge, and cry out to God, but the one thing he will not do is give up his faith. *"Curse God and die"* is the language of giving up.

At some point, life's difficulties expose whether our circumstances hold our faith or our faith holds our circumstances. This is the crossroads that Job and his wife are both brought to, and the defining difference is their response. Job's wife assumed that God had abandoned them because of their heart-wrenching circumstances. In truth, the circumstances were instigated by Satan—because of God's pride in Job—but this was information neither Job nor his wife ever knew. God's love for them had to be believed by faith, in the midst of circumstances that seemed to communicate the opposite. At the crossroads of suffering, we have to decide if we believe God's affection is defined by prosperity or if God's affection might be just as present—if not more so—in our loss.

In the story of this couple, we also witness how hardship either unites or divides us. Unfortunately for Job and his wife, they became separated by their loss. This is one of the secondary tragedies of Job's suffering. Job's wife could have chosen to sit with Job,

> At the crossroads of suffering, we have to decide if we believe God's affection is defined by prosperity or if God's affection might be just as present—if not more so—in our loss.

nurse him, pray with him, and be with him in his questions. But her stark response drove a wedge between them in how they managed their grief. Now they each had to face their suffering alone—without the comfort of each other's arms.

Since we hear no more about Job's wife after these words, we are left to speculate about what happened to her. We know she isn't present with Job in his process of coming to new spiritual understanding, so she forgoes the chance at getting an audience with God. She sentences God without questioning Him, leading her to live from her own conclusions. She represents so many people who abandon God in hardship—without giving hardship a chance to deepen their faith.

However, at the end of the book of Job, we are left to wonder if she might have actually come back.

In chapter 42 verses 12–13, Job is blessed with sheep, camels, oxen, donkeys, and more children. Scripture is silent about the woman who bore those children, but one would think there would be mention of Job's new wife if Job's old wife went away. Her words *"Curse God and die"* did not include a follow-up phrase saying that she was leaving him. Did she stay at a distance and watch? Or did she walk away from his life?

These are questions that should cause us to ponder her— past the despairing words that we know came from her. Her sentiments may have continued exactly the same—or in the silence of watching Job's journey, she *might* have evolved in her faith. Someone joined Job in chapter 42:13 and bore him ten more children. We will never know if it was her—or if she left, and Job married someone else. A phrase near the end of Job leaves room for the fact that Job's wife *may* have returned:

All his brothers and sisters and *everyone who had known him before* came and ate with him in his house. They comforted and consoled him over all the trouble the LORD had brought on him, and each one gave him a piece of silver and a gold ring.

Job 42:11 (emphasis added)

Was Job's wife included in *"everyone who had known him before"*—those who came to comfort and console him? Or did she exit stage left in chapter 2 after uttering her depressing words, never to return? Those are questions we are left with at the end of the book, as Job's prosperity is restored.

Whatever did happen, Job's wife teaches something very important about God and hardship. When we align God with prosperity and comfort, we believe God has abandoned us when prosperity and comfort are taken away. That was Satan's bet—that Job would not be able to see past his suffering to discover a God who still loved him. Instead, it was Job's wife who gave the response that Satan was looking for from Job.

The only benefit of Job's wife's words is that they triggered Job to make a commitment of resolve that must have strengthened his endurance for weeks of continued suffering. By proclaiming back to her, "Shall we accept good from God, and not trouble?" (Job 2:10), he had a question to hold in front of himself as trouble became his call. In a strange way, she provoked his faithfulness, though certainly not in the way you would hope for in a marriage. The sad truth about Job's wife is that she couldn't join Job and hold his hand in his resolve.

Personally, I hope that "everyone who knew him before" (Job 42:11) included her, and that Job's faith ended up bringing her back to him. Even more, I hope that watching his journey brought her to a new and better understanding of God. All we have is what is recorded in his story to make a speculation. But if Job's wife watched what happened and returned, I believe she had a deeper understanding of hardship when God welcomed her back.

JOHN 21: Difficulty Brings a Mature Faith

God not only takes us through hardship, but in this third passage, we see that our hardship may define our ministry. After Jesus's resurrection, when Peter is reinstated in John 21, he is called to ministry and hardship in the same breath. To give some background, just before Jesus's death, Jesus told Peter he was going to deny Him three times (see John 13:38). Peter vehemently rejected Jesus's prophetic words about him, but as soon as Jesus was arrested in John 18, Peter did exactly what Jesus said. Three times Peter proclaimed that he was not with Jesus (John 18:17, 25–27). This detail is crucial for understanding the way Jesus reinstates Peter in John 21 after He comes back from the dead.

After the disciples recognize Jesus and then eat breakfast with Him, Jesus turns to Peter and addresses him. Calling him by his birth name, Simon, Jesus asks him the same question three times. Here's how the dialogue is recorded:

> "Simon son of John, do you love me more than these?"
>
> "Yes, Lord," he said, "you know that I love you."
>
> Jesus said, "Feed my lambs."
>
> Again Jesus said, "Simon son of John, do you love me?"
>
> He answered, "Yes, Lord, you know that I love you."
>
> Jesus said, "Take care of my sheep."
>
> The third time he said to him, "Simon son of John, do you love me?"
>
> Peter was hurt because Jesus asked him the third time, "Do you love me?" He said, "Lord, you know all things; you know that I love you."
>
> Jesus said, "Feed my sheep."
>
> John 21:15–17

Three times in John 18, Peter had denied Jesus. Now three times in John 21, Peter is given the chance to proclaim his love. Peter doesn't seem to see this connection, because he is hurt when Jesus repeats the question. But if he had thought back to the number of his denials, he would have seen the tie. Sometimes we aren't even aware when God is giving us exactly what we need.

When Jesus says, "Simon son of John, do you love me more than these?" (v. 15), we can possibly deduce that "these" might have been the fish around them. Peter had gone back to fishing after being a disciple, and because he thought Jesus had died, he had resumed his former job. But now, with Jesus risen from the dead, Peter is asked anew if following Jesus will become his primary call.

After asking Peter about his love for Him, Jesus then gives him a directive for his ministry. It's our love for God that brings forth our commitment to serve, and "feed my sheep" is really what all followers of Jesus are called to do. But right after Peter's call to ministry come the more difficult words about the future that Peter will be called to endure:

> Very truly I tell you, when you were younger you dressed yourself and went where you wanted; but when you are old you will stretch out your hands, and someone else will dress you and lead you where you do not want to go.
>
> John 21:18

I've always wondered if "when you are old" is a reference to Peter's age or spiritual maturity. Certainly the latter could be argued, for it is a sign of spiritual maturity to go wherever God leads. We are not left to wonder *where* Peter is going to be led, because verse 19 clarifies Jesus's words about Peter's destiny. Peter will die at the hands of others after his ministry on earth is through. The only comfort comes in what Jesus says next: "Follow me!" (v. 19).

In a very real sense, Jesus is saying, "Peter, I'm leading you where I have gone before you. And when you are led where you do not want to go, I will be with you, because I've been there too."

In Jesus we see the manifestation of a God who suffers with us. God doesn't take our suffering away, but God goes into it *with* us, holding our hand. And if we ever doubt that God understands the depth of our suffering, the crucifixion dissolves our doubts.

"Here on earth you will have many trials and sorrows," Jesus promises His disciples, having lived what He is saying. Then He follows that dire promise with these words: "But take heart, because I have overcome the world" (John 16:33 NLT).

The promise of a new world *without* suffering is where we are going. The promise of a world *with* suffering is where we are now. But God is with us here.

I've always found humor in the first response Peter gives after this weighty charge from Jesus. As John walks by, Peter shouts out, "Lord, what about him?" (John 21:21).

When we are called to follow God into hardship, it's difficult not to look at other people's lives and wonder why they seem to have it easy. We may question why God is doing this to *us*. But suffering makes its way into every life; it just comes in different packages. We can't compare ourselves to others (especially through staged glimpses on social media) and assume we have a correct assessment of their life. Jesus's words to Peter jolt us to stop focusing on others and turn our attention back to ourselves: "If I want him to remain alive until I return, what is that to you? You must follow me" (John 21:22).

Jesus's gentle chiding reminds Peter that the only concern he should have is his own life. We shouldn't spend all our time looking at other people's lives, because it takes away from the energy that we need for the life we have. We may not have a choice about the life we are given, but we have choices every day about how we will live it. According to Jesus's words, our energy should be focused on managing our own life.

One last observation in this passage is found in Jesus's words to Peter: "When you were younger you dressed yourself and went where you wanted" (v. 18). It could be that Jesus is referring to the stage when we are new believers and we believe God's favor is upon us when things are going our way. God may accommodate us with many answers to prayers we've asked for in order to set the foundation of His attention to us. But Jesus reminds us in this dialogue with Peter that this stage is only the beginning of our spiritual growth.

As new believers, we thrill when God delivers just what we want—at exactly the time we want it. As we mature in our faith, we understand God's love is deeper than our wants—and isn't measured by things going our way. In fact, according to the passages we just read, sometimes God's love is experienced most profoundly when things *don't* go our way.

In all three stories we find God's deepest love manifested in people's hardship. Peter's story alludes to the fact that hardship is aligned with maturity in our faith. In parenting we know this is true; sometimes we withhold things our children want for the sake of their maturity. If a mother doesn't eventually wean her child off her breast, she is doing him a disservice to his growth.

Parents move children into growth by saying *no* more than *yes*, and if you are a loving parent, there will come a time (if not many times) when your child can't stand you. Only when your children become adults will they see the wisdom and love in what you did. It's not hard to imagine that our heavenly Father brings us to maturity the same way.

The more we are able to accept God's no, the stronger our faith grows, and the more we can trust when something is withheld from us. The call to "do hard" is God's call to a deeper, more meaningful faith.

The truth that we discover from Hagar, Job, and Peter is that the call to hardship is not a sign of God's displeasure. It means that God has plans for what He wants to do *in* and *through* the story of our lives that only suffering and hardship can write. Many of us realize that we touch others more through our pain rather than through our prosperity. We immediately connect to people who have experienced our same pain, and God often uses that pain to be a healing agent in other people's lives. Shared pain brings people together—we see it happen in AA meetings, cancer wards, and grief groups. And it's through Jesus's suffering that hurting people connect most deeply to God.

Our God came to earth and suffered and died to show us that hardship isn't something to be feared or avoided. The resurrection reveals that hardship can be entered and endured, because it has been overcome.

REFLECTION QUESTIONS

1. As you look at Genesis 16 and 21, God asks Hagar to go back when she didn't want to and then to leave when she had finally settled in. What does that tell you about God? Do you think He has a higher purpose than making us comfortable?

2. Job 2:9 is the only verse that speaks directly about Job's wife. After reading this chapter, do you have any more empathy for or understanding of her? How would you

have responded if you had been in her place? What does her story teach us about circumstances and faith?

3. In John 21:18–22, Jesus tells Peter he will be led where he doesn't want to go. What does that tell you about God and suffering? Do you think it is an honor or a punishment when God allows suffering in our life?

8

When in Doubt, Look at Jesus

"THE SON IS THE IMAGE of the invisible God, the firstborn over all creation" (Colossians 1:15). These words tell us where to look for God when we are plagued with doubts. Whether we are disillusioned by people who represent God, face circumstances we begged God to avoid, or feel like we are living in a world devoid of God's presence, the place to turn to rediscover God is the person who these words in Colossians describe.

"For God was pleased to have all his fullness dwell in him" verse 19 adds, and we need to remind ourselves that no one but Jesus carries the weight of this promise. Our faith falters when we attribute God's fullness to others—even if they are people we admire. When they disappoint us—which they nearly always do—we may start to question God's existence. People help point our way to God, but we can't give them the power to represent who God is. The Bible declares in Colossians 1 that only one human being has ever held God's fullness. The rest of us are a Romans 7:18 mixture of frailty and grace. As we mature in our faith, we become more aware of this truth.

As a new believer, I remember hanging on every word of my college pastor. I took piles of notes on his teaching, formed my spiritual growth under his leadership, and grew to consider a vocation in ministry because of his influence on my life. He was smart, dashing, and charismatic, a father of five, and husband to a beautiful woman we all admired. When I found out later about his unfaithfulness and sexual abuse—all during his thriving ministry—my faith tremored and was nearly unearthed.

How could I believe in a God who was represented by such hypocrisy? I wish this was an isolated example, but he was only one of many to come. From a man I knew who pioneered a huge Christian music festival and then who was caught in sexual abuse, to a bestselling Christian author turned atheist, to countless pastors and leaders marred by indiscretions, my years of being a Christian have been filled with people who left me questioning if what I believed could still be authentic. My own seasons of complacency and selfishness have made me feel like a disappointment to others too.

> When we see how Jesus loved, spoke, interacted, and healed, we find our way back to God.

It's comforting to know there is one person who existed in history who we can point to when people need a picture of God.

For every confusing Scripture passage you read, Jesus's life and ministry is where to go with your questions. For every leader who disappoints you, Jesus is the leader you can look to and trust. For every piece of evidence that seems to point to

God's absence or neglect, Jesus's stories are the place to find help for our questions. When we see how Jesus loved, spoke, interacted, and healed, we find our way back to God. In this chapter, we will look at three passages from Jesus's life that can help strengthen our faith.

MATTHEW 8: God Is Peaceful in Your Crisis

The sky filled with clouds so quickly, they had no time to turn back to shore to avoid what was happening. Waves started crashing over the sides of their boat before they could formulate a plan to survive. The crisis had caught them off guard—especially since they had followed Jesus's direction to be there. When a storm came over this particular lake, it swept in with little to no forewarning—you just had to brace yourself and try to outlast its force.

This lake was known as the Sea of Galilee, and it is where the disciples fished and boated, so they knew its unpredictable behavior. With high hills surrounding water well below sea level, abrupt temperature changes made sudden storms a common event.[1] Sometimes storms would pass as quickly as they came, but their force could not be contained or regulated. For people in small boats, these storms could be deadly, and this one caused the disciples to question whether they would survive.

In the midst of the storm's chaos, when they looked at Jesus, He was sleeping. They probably stared at Him for a moment in disbelief, then their desperate cries shook Him awake: "Lord, save us! We're going to drown!" (Matthew 8:25).

I don't know about you, but I have lived this scene in times when God seemed asleep or absent. Something happened in

1. Ray Vander Laan, "Sea of Galilee Geography," That the World May Know, https://www.thattheworldmayknow.com/sea-of-galilee-geography.

my life that shocked and overwhelmed me, and in that moment, I couldn't see any sign of God's help. It's especially confusing when God seems to be silent and, instead of rushing to our aid, appears to be indifferent. Jesus's nap during the disciples' crisis seems to be no accident in the way it speaks to the storms of our lives.

When Jesus was awakened, verse 26 states that He scolded the weather. In Mark's account, Jesus's words to the wind and waves are unpretentiously profound: "He got up, rebuked the wind and said to the waves, 'Quiet! Be still!'" (Mark 4:39).

The disciples were shocked and likely scandalized—for their teacher to be commanding the wind and waves, He was taking them a big step forward in what they had experienced from Him. They had been amazed by His healings, but this was their first glimpse of His otherworldly force. Even more shocking was what happened next: the wind and the waves responded to Him. With their mouths still open, Jesus addresses His disciples with a question that is recorded in both Matthew's and Mark's accounts: "Why are you so afraid? Do you still have no faith?" (Mark 4:40).

Well, yes, Jesus, we had faith, but this just took our faith to a different altitude. That response is not in the Bible, but I imagine something like it was swirling around in their heads. They couldn't even respond because they were silenced by His power. Instead, they questioned everything they thought they knew, because of what they had just seen.

"What kind of man is this?" (Matthew 8:27) they whispered, which is an interesting question from people who had already decided to follow Him. The person they were following had grown exponentially larger in their midst.

This is the first account from Jesus's life that exposes the direct connection between God and Jesus. Prior to this, Jesus had healed, taught, and driven out demons, but commanding the weather took the disciples' understanding of His power to a new height. The disciples now knew they were in the presence of God, and the humble package God had come in took them, and many others, by surprise.

After Jesus displayed this power, the gospel of Mark says that the disciples were terrified, while the gospel of Matthew says they were amazed by Him. These words are interchangeable when we are in the presence of something that leaves us both astounded and aghast. Jesus scared the disciples, as well as thrilled them, with this display and reach of His power. When they got to the other side of the lake after it happened, their faith was changed by what they had seen.

This passage reaches into our crises by illustrating—through Jesus—where God is when it feels like He is absent. When it seems like God is sleeping, it's because the crisis is well inside His care and command. God may even *lead* us into crisis, just as Jesus led His disciples into the boat, but God always has a plan for what happens. We can't see God's power over a storm unless we are in the storm when it takes place. By sleeping, Jesus extravagantly models the peace we can have no matter what crisis is occurring. Jesus is under the same threat as His disciples in this storm, yet He naps to display His nonchalance. By watching His peace, we can find our own.

When Jesus says, "You of little faith" (Matthew 8:26), He is letting the disciples know that they didn't understand the fullness of His dominion. They had not yet realized they had a God who reigned over their circumstances and that His presence with them was their power. Jesus held the same authority while He napped as He did when He waved the storm away from them. By displaying His power in each of these actions, Jesus shows us something different and important about God.

> The peace we have does not come when the crisis is removed; it's available to us *while the crisis is happening.*

Through this story, we see that the peace we have does not come when the crisis is removed; it's available to us *while the crisis is happening.* Peace is different from joy—it's the understanding that no matter what happens, or how bad things may feel, God is in control. Whether God stops the storm or holds us through it, our confidence is not in what happens with our circumstances, but in God's presence. In this remarkable story, Jesus makes it clear that God holds the power behind everything that happens, and we can rest in that assurance in the midst of fear or grief.

God's presence is our peace.

MARK 2: God Acts Unpredictably in Your Need

The four of them knew what they wanted, and they weren't going to let anything deter them. They made that clear as they dug through the roof in the middle of Jesus's teaching, when debris started falling near Jesus's head. They hadn't been able to get their friend through the crowd, so they came up with this plan to lower him down on a mat to get close to Him. This was their one and only chance to get their paralyzed friend close enough to Jesus to get the healing they felt he deserved.

They knew Jesus as a healer, but if they peered down through the roof as they dug, they could see there was more to Him. He taught in a way that captivated crowds, and delivered His words with such power, the friends likely felt hopeful that their request would be received. It's likely they didn't realize until they got there that it would be too crowded to carry their paralyzed friend up close to Him. It's anyone's guess whether the homeowner condoned (or had any idea about) their plan.

The passage skips those details and fast-forwards to the moment the four friends lowered their friend down through the roof in front of Jesus. We can only imagine how self-conscious the man must have felt. He had spent his life unable to move from being sidelined. Now he found himself inadvertently taking center stage, wondering—along with everyone else—what would happen next.

He may have wondered if he'd be condemned because of his friends' bold—and arguably rude—behavior. However, his appreciation for them likely overruled his embarrassment; he had friends who cared so deeply about him, they were willing to take this risk.

When the man finally got to the floor, all eyes were on Jesus; however, Mark 2:5 says that Jesus's eyes were on the friends who brought the man to Him. The verse says that when Jesus saw their faith, He turned to the man on the mat, while everyone waited for His response.

"Son, your sins are forgiven" (Mark 2:5).

I imagine Jesus's words hung in the air, with an awkward silence. The passage makes it clear that the Pharisees in the back of the house squirmed, but the man's friends on the roof must have been stunned. *Your sins are forgiven? Did He think this is what we came for?* Wasn't it obvious that the reason they had gone to such extremes is because they wanted their friend to walk?

These reactions are only speculation; the passage leaves us to interpret what happened between these words and what Mark next recorded. Verse 6 describes the reactions of the Pharisees, but the man's friends aren't mentioned again after Jesus affirmed their faith in the previous verse. However, it is not hard to imagine that, for a moment, they thought their efforts might have been a waste.

Or maybe they realized Jesus saw something that they couldn't see, something even more important than walking. Certainly the reaction of the teachers of the law indicated that what Jesus said was way more scandalous than telling the paralyzed man to get up and walk. Verses 6 and 7 say the Pharisees condemned Jesus for blasphemy, because they knew only God could offer this forgiveness. What they couldn't see is that this is exactly why Jesus could do what He did.

We don't know anything about the background of this man's paralysis—if he thought his condition was because of something he did, if it was a condition he was born with, or if it happened in an accident. Mark doesn't include those details, but it appears that Jesus is intentional in choosing words of forgiveness as the first words He said. Somehow, they must have been words the man, as well as the Pharisees, needed to hear.

Jesus knows what the teachers of the law are thinking, so He responds, "Why are you thinking these things?" Then He asks them, "Which is easier: to say to this paralyzed man, 'Your sins are forgiven,' or to say, 'Get up, take your mat and walk'?" (Mark 2:8–9).

Before the teachers of the law have a chance to answer, Jesus adds something else, and His next words must have particularly made the Pharisees squirm: "'So I will prove to you that the Son of Man has the authority on earth to forgive sins.' Then Jesus turned to the paralyzed man and said, 'Stand up, pick up your mat, and go home!'" (Mark 2:10–11 NLT).

Jesus not only had the audacity to forgive the paralyzed man's sins, He used the healing as an opportunity to showcase His spiritual authority. Before telling the man to walk, Jesus makes it clear that this healing will reveal He has the same authority as God. If Jesus had kept this event strictly as a physical healing, the Pharisees might have left the scene admiring Him. But because Jesus proclaimed His authority to spiritually heal people too, this event became the first of many that the Pharisees would condemn.

The next verse makes it clear that everyone in that house witnessed what happened. The paralyzed man got up, took his mat, and *"walked out in full view of them all"* (Mark 2:12, emphasis added). Though they were likely astonished by what they saw of the man's physical healing, Jesus made it clear that it was what the people *couldn't* see that the man needed most.

In this passage, Jesus reveals that while we are captivated by healing that is physical, God prioritizes healing that is internal. Physical healing is dramatic and miraculous, while spiritual healing is often inward and invisible, and our tendency is to weigh the impact by what we see. However, the real scale should measure what endures the longest, and spiritual healing outlasts our bodies. Our greatest healings take place under the surface, and they are what lead to significant and lasting change. The result of spiritual healing is what happens in and through people after the healing takes place.

When people experience inner peace after a lifetime of turmoil, it not only changes their countenance but their influence on others. When people receive undeserved forgiveness from God, it gives them a reservoir to extend that kind of forgiveness, which changes relationships and lives. These changes aren't seen the moment they happen, but the ripple effect of spiritual healing is more significant than physical healing.

Looking deeper into which kind of healing is more prevailing, most of us would agree that spiritual healing carries more force.

> The faith we carry for our friends may be more significant than we imagine.

We also learn in this passage that the faith we carry for our friends may be more significant than we imagine. It was the man's friends' faith that inspired Jesus to heal the man (v. 5), so we shouldn't discount the faith we hold for friends who need hope. It can feel like a waste of time when we don't see any impact from our prayers and longing. This story reveals that it may take perseverance to hold those prayers before God. We need to persist in loving and praying for our friends; in time, God might take our prayer and use it to change someone's life.

It's hard to assess who is the biggest star of this story in Mark 2—the friends, the paralyzed man, or Jesus. All three are cheered and commended, and that gives us our last insight about God. When God's work is seen, and we are a part of it, God takes delight in sharing the spotlight. Because God uses us to bring His kingdom to earth, Jesus shows in this story that God is more than willing to share the applause.

And no applause is sweeter to receive than the praise that erupts from the work of God.

LUKE 8: God's Agenda Is Different from Yours

Jairus was a synagogue ruler, so he was used to people gathering around him. But in this passage, he humbly falls at Jesus's feet—pleading for something outside of his control. Though Jairus was in charge of the place where people came to worship, his daughter's sickness confronted him with his powerlessness. His need for healing placed him alongside everyone else, and he joined the multitudes who came to Jesus for healing, begging for Jesus's help.

Luke 8:41–42 says Jairus was pleading with Jesus because he knew his twelve-year-old daughter was dying. Verse 42 includes the detail that she was his only daughter, making the stakes of her healing immeasurably high. Jairus's status is evident in the crowds that almost crushed Jesus as they followed Him toward Jairus's home, where his little girl lay failing

(v. 42). The scene paints Jesus submerged in a sea of bodies, all clamoring for a view of what He was going to do.

In the midst of the traveling, growing mob, the next verses say this: "And a woman was there who had been subject to bleeding for twelve years, but no one could heal her. She came up behind him and touched the edge of his cloak, and immediately her bleeding stopped" (Luke 8:43–44).

One would expect that the crowd moved on without noticing, which they might have done, if Jesus hadn't stopped and drawn attention to what happened to Him. His words undoubtedly drew a laugh, because He asked a question that, given the setting, must have seemed impossible to resolve.

"Who touched me?" Jesus asked (v. 45).

With the question hanging in the air, Peter says the obvious: "Master, the people are crowding and pressing against you." But Jesus insists, "Someone touched me; I know that power has gone out from me" (vv. 45–46), and it is clear He won't be subdued.

The desperate woman was discovered, and we can only imagine her thoughts in this unforeseen moment. Surely, she must have thought her touch would go unnoticed, given the number of people who were hanging on Jesus when she reached out. But there was something about her touch that had caused Jesus to stop.

We have to pause in this moment of the story and consider Jairus, who must have been desperate to hurry through this inquiry. His daughter was already living on borrowed time, and it was just a matter of hours before she would be gone. Now he watched as Jesus conducted an interview to find the person who had received His power.

A man used to commanding attention was relegated to the sidelines. A woman used to being hidden in the crowd was brought into the spotlight for everyone to see. Here Jesus shows us that at any given moment, God's agenda might be deeper and more layered than we think.

The passage goes on to say that "the woman, seeing that she could not go unnoticed, came trembling and fell at his feet" (v. 47), just like Jairus had done at the beginning. Verse 47 goes on to say, "In the presence of all the people, she told why she had touched him and how she had been instantly healed." Mark 5 gives a parallel account, and in verse 33, Mark writes that she "told him the whole truth," indicating that it probably took some time.

However long her "whole truth" took, both passages are clear in what happened next:

> While Jesus was still speaking, someone came from the house of Jairus, the synagogue leader. "Your daughter is dead," he said. "Don't bother the teacher anymore." Hearing this, Jesus said to Jairus, "Don't be afraid; just believe, and she will be healed."
>
> Luke 8:49–50

Jesus pushed Jairus past what he was looking for; he had wanted Jesus to heal his daughter. What Jesus was asking him to believe was out of the realm of what Jairus knew was possible, now that his daughter was dead. Even if Jairus was a good man, I imagine he harbored feelings of anger toward the woman who had inadvertently hijacked his healing. She got what he had wanted for his daughter, and now Jesus was placating him with an impossible request. How could he believe in something that he knew couldn't be done?

I'm sure Jairus barely limped behind Jesus toward his house—which now held his dead daughter. When they got there, Jesus told the crowd to remain outside and only let Peter, James, John, Jairus, and Jarius's wife follow him in. A cacophony of mourning sounds surrounded them as Jesus calmly told them to stop wailing. Jesus must have caused some people to consider Him utterly mad with what He said next: "She is not dead but asleep" (v. 52).

The passage says the mourners couldn't help but laugh at Him because they had been with her dead body for some time. I imagine Jairus held on to Jesus's words with a parent's desperate hope that what seemed to be unfolding before him would not end the way it looked. When Jesus spoke again, Jairus witnessed something far beyond anything he could have hoped.

With the words, "My child, get up!" (v. 54), Jairus's daughter's spirit returned to her. When she stood up, Jesus casually told Jairus and his wife to get her something to eat. Verse 56 states the obvious: they "were astonished," but Jesus told them not to share with anyone what had happened. This was a private miracle just for Jairus and his family, and Jesus wanted no one else to know.

A public healing and a private one, each done for two people who thought they would get the opposite. Jairus thought his daughter would be healed in front of the crowd who followed him home; the woman thought she would get her healing privately and that no one would know. It seems clear that Jesus saw needs that were beyond what was apparent, and the way He healed was as significant as the healings. The timing and way these healings happened caused both people to experience something deeper than they asked.

The bleeding woman was given the gift of importance, so along with her physical healing, she received the bonus of emotional healing. Jairus was given the experience of having to wait and trust—and because of that, he got to witness the kind of miracle very few would see. The woman experienced an upgraded reputation; the crowd that had previously ignored her saw how she captivated Jesus's attention. Jairus got to see that Jesus was much more than a healer; he was able to witness God's resurrection power at work. From this point on, Jairus would have to reconcile what he saw with what the Pharisees around him were saying about Jesus. He had experienced first-hand in his own life what Jesus could do.

What Jesus shows us about God's timing is that when God seems too slow, He might be making room for something bigger than we wanted. Jairus wanted a healing, but instead got a resurrection, because Jesus was too late to do what Jairus had asked. It's similar to what happens in John 11, when Jesus received a message from Mary and Martha to come at once to heal His friend Lazarus. Jesus waited two more days, because He had more in mind than what Mary and Martha had asked. Jesus ended up raising Lazarus from the dead, and like the res-urrection of Jairus's daughter in this passage, His delay made room for a greater miracle. From these two passages, we can surmise that God takes liberty in the timing of answering our prayers when He has more in mind than what we prayed.

> What Jesus shows us about God's timing is that when God seems too slow, He might be making room for something bigger than we wanted.

A glimpse into many mysteries of God is embedded in this small story of a bleeding woman and a synagogue ruler's daughter. This passage, along with so many others, reveals to us through Je-sus's actions the way God works. No one in this passage got what they wanted in the way they wanted it, but everyone got more than they imagined. From the woman, to Jairus, to the crowd, each got a taste of God's glory that was custom-made to strengthen their faith. There was discomfort in each of their blessings—the woman was forced out of hiding, Jairus was forced to wait, and the crowd was forced to listen to someone they deemed unimportant. But the discomfort each one experienced led to spiritual growth.

We may be focused on what is in front of us, but God has His eye on more than that. The way Jesus ministers to each person individually in this passage reveals how God can work in multiple ways in multiple people, all at once. What happens to one person often has an impact on another person, illustrating God's ability to weave our stories together in a way that impacts each one of us. No person has God's focus more than another, yet each of us has God's focus in a completely personal way. The bigness and smallness of Jesus's attention in this passage illustrates the attentive way God works.

In all three of these stories, Jesus gives us a glimpse behind the mysteries of God that we frequently ponder. The first story speaks to us when we feel abandoned in our crisis; the second, when prayers are answered differently than we asked; and the third, when God's ways and timing seem out of whack. Jesus reveals that what seems to be is not necessarily all that is happening. God may be with us when we don't feel His presence, God may be answering our prayer with more than we wanted, and God's timing may be making room for something bigger than we asked. Certainly that was true in these three stories, and when we hover over the particulars, we find comfort and insight for our own stories. The way Jesus works gives us our clearest picture of God.

REFLECTION QUESTIONS

1. Have you ever felt like the disciples in Matthew 8:23–27? At what time (or in what circumstance) has it felt like God was asleep? Is there a situation in your life

where you feel God is sleeping right now? What does this passage teach you about God's presence?

2. In Mark 2, four people bring their friend to Jesus with an agenda for Him to heal their friend's paralysis. Have you ever had an agenda in a prayer request that was answered differently than you prayed? What insight does this story give you into how God works in our lives?

3. Luke 8:40–56 tells us the story of a bleeding woman and a synagogue ruler. Which of these two people do you relate to the most in this passage? Why? How does Jesus's approach with them speak to you?

9

Find Your Compass in Community

"IT IS NOT GOOD FOR THE MAN to be alone," God says, and it is the first time the words "not good" are used about creation (Genesis 2:18). This is the earliest evidence that community is fundamental to a healthy life. God follows His proclamation by creating the first community with a woman and a man, brought together to support and help each other. Almost immediately we see the influence they have over each other, when the two of them are presented with their first choice. The serpent in Genesis 3:1 tests the woman and the man with the only thing God told them to refrain from, and this is their opportunity to help each other trust the words of their Maker. Instead, they allow each other to fall prey to their doubts, and then suffer the consequences of their choice. In the first three chapters of the Bible, we already see how our community—for good or for bad—shapes our faith.

In Genesis 1:26 (NLT), God says, "Let us make human beings in our image," so God didn't just create community, God is intrinsically communal. Since we have been created in God's image and likeness, it is inbred in us for community to shape our identity and our life. God created man and woman partly for the purpose of having children and becoming a family, setting the stage for community to surround us from the first breath of our being. The family we are born or brought into is the first and strongest influence in forming our beliefs.

Through time, however, our family's influence on our faith (or non-faith) is negotiable. Stop for a moment and consider the weight your parents (or the people who raised you) had on what you believed as a child, and how much they influence your beliefs right now. Our parents initially shape what we believe, but we reinforce or repel their influence with the community we choose to surround us. When we reach adolescence, our friends, teachers, and mentors begin to have more influence on how our beliefs are shaped. As adults, we continue to choose what community will influence us. This is one of the most important decisions you will make for the future of your faith.

> Our community— for good or for bad—shapes our faith.

Since none of us chooses our family of origin, this chapter's passages will focus on our chosen community. Whether you were born into a legacy of faith or a family filled with atheists, *the community you choose* from your teenage years forward is largely up to you. If you want to grow in your faith, you need people who are living out their faith with you. Whether or not you'll be influenced by your community is not up for debate; the people around you *will* have an impact on growing or shrinking your faith.

In this chapter, we will look at six passages instead of three, because I want to explore the contrast between a good and bad community. We will look at two passages side by side and see how people were influenced by their community in their decisions of faith. For better or for worse, people around you make a difference—not only in what you believe, but in how you live your belief.

NUMBERS 13 vs. ACTS 2: The Company You Keep Can Determine Your Destiny

These first two passages open with two communities facing a decision. One is weighing the obstacles of a God-given opportunity; the other is determining whether a miraculous event actually happened. In both stories, the community's response to the decision sealed their fate. What happened to the people in these communities serves as a warning and an encouragement about who we choose to influence our faith.

In Numbers 13, twelve spies are sent to assess the land that God promised to the Israelites, and when they return, they give their report to the Israelite community. Their job was to see what the land was like, so they could help Moses and the Israelite leaders come up with a strategy to take what was already theirs. They weren't sent to decide *if* they should go in, but *how*; their report was supposed to help the Israelites' strategy. They started out on task, but as they spoke, you can see how their report took a turn that shriveled everyone's faith. Here were their words:

> We went into the land to which you sent us, and it does flow with milk and honey! Here is its fruit. But the people who live there are powerful, and the cities are fortified and very large. We even saw descendants of Anak there. The Amalekites live

in the Negev; the Hittites, Jebusites and Amorites live in the hill country; and the Canaanites live near the sea and along the Jordan.

Numbers 13:27–29

I've read these words multiple times, and I can't help but wonder what would have happened if they ended their report with "Here is its fruit" (v. 27). Perhaps the disaster that ensued after they gave their report could have been avoided if they hadn't let their fear color their words. Caleb tries to silence them with words of faith that contrasted what the other spies were saying: "We should go up and take possession of the land, for we can certainly do it" (v. 30). But the community needed to act on these words to experience their truth.

Unfortunately, ten spies contradict Caleb's encouragement with a statement (born from fear) that fills everyone with doubt: "We can't attack those people; they are stronger than we are" (v. 31).

If the community had stopped and reaffirmed what God had already told them, perhaps they would have searched their hearts and sided with Caleb. But the spies spread their bad report among the rest of the Israelite community, telling everyone they would be devoured by giants if they dared to take the land. Here's what happened next:

All the Israelites grumbled against Moses and Aaron, and the whole assembly said to them, "If only we had died in Egypt! Or in this wilderness! Why is the Lord bringing us to this land only to let us fall by the sword?"

Numbers 14:2–3

Like the evolution of a story in a game of Telephone, the land had evolved to something different from what it actually was because of the way people conversed about it. From a land filled with milk and honey, it turned into a land of man-eating giants as the spies convinced the Israelites not to take what God had promised was already theirs. Their report ended with the perfect words to inflame everyone's fear: "We seemed like grasshoppers in our own eyes, and we looked the same to them" (Numbers 13:33).

Watching how fear took over the course of the Israelites' journey, we observe the power of community. The people you surround yourself with are crucial to how you live your faith. If the people had listened to Caleb, this story would not have ended in tragedy. This passage shows how the influence of the wrong community has the power to derail our faith.

In contrast to Numbers 13, Acts 2 describes what happens when a community responds to a situation with faith, and spreads it to the people around them. The Holy Spirit descends on a group of believers, and when some of them start speaking in other languages, outsiders stop to listen in. As people hear their native tongue spoken by people who aren't from their country, more and more people gather around them in astonishment. There were two opinions on what was happening, which was evident from their response: "Amazed and perplexed, they asked one another, 'What does this mean?' Some, however, made fun of them and said, 'They have had too much wine'" (vv. 12–13).

Like we witnessed in Numbers 13, there were voices of doubt present in the community. However, the difference in Acts 2 is which voices the community allowed to lead them—which in turn shaped the group's response. Like Caleb in Numbers 13, Peter stands up to address the crowd, but in this passage, the community actually listens to him. Peter was given the floor to speak longer than Caleb, and his words compelled the attention of the crowd. He tells them this isn't drunkenness but the work of the Holy Spirit, who was sent by Jesus. What is interesting is how the crowd's response to Peter's words impacted what happened next: "They were cut to the heart and said to Peter and the other apostles, 'Brothers, what shall we do?'" (Acts 2:37).

Because of their open hearts, when Peter tells them to repent and be baptized, *three thousand people* were baptized and added to their number (v. 41). The community grew exponentially because of their response, and it became a very different community from the one in Numbers 13. Here is the description of the way the Acts 2 community lived:

> They devoted themselves to the apostles' teaching and to fellowship, to the breaking of bread and to prayer. Everyone was filled with awe at the many wonders and signs performed by the apostles. All the believers were together and had everything in common. They sold property and possessions to give to anyone who had need.
>
> Acts 2:42–45

Where fear breeds insecurity, doubt, and division, faith breeds support, sacrifice, and miracles. A community can lead people either way—depending on what voices are empowered to guide the community's response. Caleb tried to silence the spies in Numbers 13 and speak words of faith, but he was drowned out by voices of fear that grew in number and eventually gained more power. As more people were influenced by fright and doubt, the community became toxic to the Israelites' faith.

Conversely, the community in Acts 2 listened to Peter and responded with faith in action. As they grew through teaching, fellowship, and generosity, more people were drawn to join in. Verse 47 says, "The Lord added to their number daily those who were being saved," partly because the Acts 2 community was a place where people didn't just speak about faith, they lived it. Because of the way they lived and supported each other, they witnessed many miraculous signs and wonders, which grew their faith. What a contrast to the community of Numbers 13, who wandered for forty years worrying and complaining. Both communities shaped the people who were a part of them—either by nurturing or dissolving their faith.

As a footnote, among the entire group of Israelites in Numbers 13, only two people—Caleb and Joshua—entered the promised land, because they stood apart from their community and believed God would fulfill His promises. Conversely, the entire community of Acts 2 experienced signs, wonders, and strength in unity, because the people chose *together* to listen to Peter and respond in faith. For better or for worse, our community often ends up directing the path of our lives; deciding what voices we will let influence

> Where fear breeds insecurity, doubt, and division, faith breeds support, sacrifice, and miracles.

us may be a bigger decision than we imagine. The people we listen to can change our destiny—so we should think clearly about our choice.

The next two passages emphasize that truth.

MATTHEW 27 vs. 2 SAMUEL 12: Listening to Truth Guards Your Heart

When we are confronted with something we don't want to face, it is tempting to reject those who confront us, because their words lead to discomfort. Having people in our lives who tell us the truth forces us to acknowledge what we want to avoid or pushes us to take action that we might resist. Whether or not we listen to these voices might make the difference in how our life turns out.

The story of Pontius Pilate is one of the most tragic accounts in the New Testament. He is the Roman governor who ultimately decided to sentence Jesus to death. Though he attempted repeatedly to absolve himself of this responsibility, his name is recited in the Apostles' Creed as the person who orchestrated Jesus's suffering. It is terribly ironic that Pilate tried everything he could to liberate himself of this decision, yet he bears the responsibility for sending Jesus to His death. The crowd that Pilate felt compelled to please sealed his fate.

Matthew 27 records the last conversation between Pilate and Jesus. Pilate begins by asking Jesus point-blank about His kingship. "So You are the King of the Jews?" (v. 11 NASB) he asks, and Jesus doesn't beat around the bush, responding directly, "It is as you say."

It's a clear statement that Pilate could have responded to, but Pilate changes the subject and asks Jesus why He's not answering the accusations that have been made about Him. Pilate is too conflicted to proclaim Jesus's innocence, even though he suspects it's true, because he can't take a stand against the crowd. It's almost as if he wants Jesus to do it for him by refuting the crowd's accusations, which Jesus will not accommodate. So Pilate tries another approach—he presents the crowd with a decision that he believes will be a sure deal.

"Which one do you want me to release to you—Barabbas, or Jesus who is called the Messiah?" (Matthew 27:17 NLT) Pilate shouts, and when he first asks this question, the crowd is silent. Verse 18 gives us a peek into Pilate's thoughts; he knew that Jesus had been handed over because of envy, so he likely thinks they'll choose Barabbas to be sentenced to death. Even though Pilate is compelled by Jesus's innocence, he isn't strong enough to go against the crowd to make a judgment. He puts the decision in their hands—and they call for Barabbas to be released.

Matthew 27:19 includes a detail that is not included in the other gospels: Pilate's wife had a troubling dream about Jesus and sends Pilate an urgent message that he shouldn't have anything to do with him because he is innocent. Her note affirms what Pilate seems to know deep inside. So Pilate has not only heard Jesus confirm His kingship, he also has his wife's urging—yet his need for popularity overrules their voices. You can feel Pilate's conflict because of the number of times he turns to the crowd.

Pilate can't act on the truth two important people have shown him. But making no decision is in fact a decision; Pilate's inability to affirm the truth paves the way for Jesus to be condemned. Pilate cannot do what he knows is right because he is too concerned about his reputation. This ironically seals his reputation for all time as the one who sent Jesus to the cross.

The passage in John adds a rhetorical question, which ultimately defines Pilate's dilemma. When Jesus says, "Everyone on the side of truth listens to me," Pilate retorts, "What is truth?" (John 18:37–38), and Jesus lets the question hang in the air. This is the question Pilate tries to hide behind, never admitting he believes in Jesus but unwilling to take a stand for or against Him. Yet no matter how many times Pilate asks the crowd why they are sparing a criminal over Jesus, the crowd pushes Pilate to sentence Jesus to death. He cannot get the crowd to do what he isn't strong enough to do himself.

Pilate's dilemma is painful to read because you can feel his reluctance to own his thoughts and actions. His story reveals what happens when we can't do what we know we should do and end up holding the consequences of a decision we tried not to make.

Second Samuel 12 tells a different story, documenting the confrontation between Nathan and David after David's fall with Bathsheba. Though we looked briefly at David's fall in chapter 3, I want to focus on some of the hard truth Nathan spoke to David, and how David responds. Nathan begins by telling David an allegory about a rich man and a poor shepherd—but he is interrupted when David becomes incensed and condemns the rich man. Nathan turns to David and says, "You are the man!" (v. 7) and the severe words that follow that proclamation must have pierced David's heart:

> Why did you despise the word of the LORD by doing what is evil in his eyes? You struck down Uriah the Hittite with the sword and took his wife to be your own. You killed him with the sword of the Ammonites. Now, therefore, the sword will never depart from your house, because you despised me and took the wife of Uriah the Hittite to be your own.
>
> 2 Samuel 12:9–10

David could have responded by denying responsibility for Uriah's death, because he technically did not hold the sword that killed him. He gave the order for Uriah to be sent to the front lines of battle, but David was not the one who put Uriah to death. However, David does not hide behind those details; instead he takes full ownership of his sinful behavior. His response is repentant, brief, and simply stated; he is direct and contrite.

"I have sinned against the LORD" (2 Samuel 12:13).

Unlike Pilate, David listens to the truth—even though it will cost him his reputation to agree with it—and he boldly and contritely responds to it. This solidifies his reputation, despite this tragic mistake, as a man after God's own heart.

Because of David's soft heart in responding to the voice of truth, he receives God's forgiveness. But it is clear from Nathan's words that David will not escape the consequences of what he has done. Being king, David could have refused to listen to Nathan's harsh sentence of what was going to happen to him and his family. Instead, David received Nathan's words in silence and remorse.

David goes on after this encounter to fast and pray (v. 16), and when the child that he and Bathsheba conceived passes away, David goes to Bathsheba to comfort her (v. 24). Facing the consequences of his actions must have caused David immeasurable pain, but hearing—and responding to—the truth set him free.

Pilate, on the other hand, avoided responding to the truth by letting the crowd control his decision. Then Pilate was left with the job of sentencing Jesus, so the decision he desperately tried to avoid was the choice that defined his life. It's interesting to look at the difference between David's and Pilate's actions after being confronted with voices of truth: David confesses, repents, and fasts (2 Samuel 12:13–16), whereas Pilate washes his hands in front of the crowd and claims his innocence (Matthew 27:24). These responses illustrate who we become after we own or avoid the truth.

> The people we choose to listen to may lead us to a response that defines our life.

David is remembered as a man after God's own heart (1 Samuel 13:14), because he owned the truth even when the truth humiliated him. Pilate is remembered as the one under whom Jesus suffered, because he couldn't respond to the truth he knew deep inside. They each show in different ways how important it is to listen to voices of truth, and this is a critical attribute of our community. The people we choose to listen to may lead us to a response that defines our life.

EXODUS 17 vs. ACTS 4: Faith Is Strengthened by Holding Your Stories

The right community strengthens our faith, encourages us to face the truth, and helps us hold on to our stories of God's faithfulness. The wrong community weakens our faith, allows us to live in deception, and distorts our memory of what God did. Our community influences how we remember God's work in our lives, which alters the way we respond to challenges in our faith.

Exodus 17 tells of the Israelites' continuing saga in the wilderness; their inability to remember God's faithfulness now permeated the community. They initially revealed their memory lapse when they complained about having no food just after watching the Red Sea part; now, after watching God provide food from the sky, they are crying out to Moses because they have nothing to drink. Their question in Exodus 17:3 shows how their litany of faithlessness continued to fill the air: "Why did you bring us up out of Egypt to make us and our children and livestock die of thirst?"

Their words are strangely similar to the exact same verse number in the previous chapter, when in their hunger they remembered Egypt as a place where they sat around eating "all the food [they] wanted" (Exodus 16:3). At that time it had been only a month and a half after God rescued them from slavery, and they had already forgotten the misery they endured while they were there. Their memory skipped over God's faithfulness in rescuing them, and they selectively remembered the food they ate while they were slaves in Egypt. Now, after being fed in the desert, they believe they are going to die of thirst. This Israelite community had severe memory issues when it came to their stories of faith.

You can sense Moses's exasperation when he cries out to God, "What am I to do with these people? They are almost ready to stone me" (Exodus 17:4).

The Lord tells Moses to strike a rock to provide water, and it miraculously flows out of the rock in front of them. Unsurprisingly, there is no appreciative response from the crowd. Instead, these are the Israelites' words in Exodus 17:7: "Is the LORD among us or not?"

Huh?

If they had remembered *anything* from their past, that question had already been answered multiple times—first and foremost when God split the sea after orchestrating the exodus. After watching God part a sea in front of them, that question never should have emerged from their lips again. Manna from the sky had proved God's presence again, yet the Israelite community seemed plagued by the inability to remember their faith stories. They should have been proclaiming to each other all the things God had done for them; instead, they filled each other with doubt. The community that should have been nothing but confident, based on what God had repeatedly done, could not believe God was capable of doing it again.

A very different story is found in Acts 4, which is the continuing saga of the Acts 2 community. Now facing some hardship, this community's response was completely different from the Israelites in Exodus 17. Peter and John had been put in jail by the Sanhedrin, and after they were released, they were commanded to never again speak about Jesus. The chief priests had let Peter and John go, but it was clear they would punish them if they didn't stop. When Peter and John reported the Sanhedrin's warning to their community, instead of being fearful, the community sought confidence through their faith memories, which they proclaimed in prayer.

They begin their prayer by remembering God's sovereign power, saying, "You made the heavens and the earth and the sea, and everything in them" (Acts 4:24). They move on to proclaim the power of the Holy Spirit in the past, then ask for strength to keep speaking by the power of the Holy Spirit now—and to continue healing and performing miracles in Jesus's name (vv. 25–30). Verse 31 says that as a result of this prayer, the entire community was strengthened, and they were able to speak even more boldly about Jesus to others. The next verses describe what the community looked like because of the way they reaffirmed and held on to their faith:

> All the believers were one in heart and mind. No one claimed that any of their possessions was their own, but they shared everything they had. With great power the apostles continued to testify to the resurrection of the Lord Jesus. And God's grace was so powerfully at work in them all . . .
>
> Acts 4:32–33

What a difference this group of believers was from the group in Exodus. The Acts 4 community was defined by grace and hospitality, whereas the Exodus 17 community was defined by quarreling and complaints. In Exodus 17:7, Moses even re-names the place where the Israelites camped "Massah" and "Meribah" (meaning "testing" and "quarreling")—their journey was literally marked by their complaining. Even though the Israelite community had the manna in front of them to remind them of God's faithfulness (Exodus 16:34), they chose to focus on their doubts. The multiple times they longed to go back to Egypt show how skewed their faith memory had become. Returning to slavery seemed more comfortable than trusting God to provide.

On the other hand, the community in Acts 4 seemed to thrive in hardship because they held fast to their faith memories. They also remembered how God worked after it looked like Jesus had been defeated on the cross. The Acts 4 community repeated Scriptures that illustrated God's power over past circumstances, and then they claimed that same power for their present hardship.

They used an excerpt from Psalm 2 to strengthen the community's faith: "Why do the nations rage and the peoples plot in vain? The kings of the earth rise up and the rulers band together against the Lord and against his anointed one" (Acts 4:25–26). Then they prayed that the same God who overcame leaders in the past would overcome the earthly leaders they faced now.

The Scripture and stories they included in their prayer in Acts 4:24–30 are a model for us in remembering our faith stories. The community recounts past events that point to God's faithfulness; then they claim that same faithfulness in their present circumstances.

Reciting this prayer gave people renewed confidence, instead of feeding their fears about what might happen. When Peter and John returned from being arrested, they knew the chief priests might try to arrest them again. If the community didn't stay quiet, the Sanhedrin might even come and arrest all of them. But instead of huddling in fear and staying silent, they proclaimed God's faithfulness in prayer, which empowered them to continue to speak.

After they prayed, the Holy Spirit came down and shook the room (v. 31), and they spoke the word of God fearlessly. They continued to boldly testify to Jesus's resurrection, and because they trusted God for His provision, they were able to share with one another everything they had (vv. 32–35). This is the kind of community you want if you want to live by faith.

From these six passages we can observe the power of the people around us—not only in shaping our faith but our future. The people we surround ourselves with carry more power to direct our actions and decisions than we might think. David

> The voices we listen to not only will impact our faith, they will shape our character and reputation.

and Pilate show us that the voices we listen to not only will impact our faith, they will shape our character and reputation. Listening—or not listening—to people who speak truth to our souls can make or break who we become.

Watching how the community from Exodus and Numbers continued to evolve—as they repeatedly chose to complain and doubt—warns us about what we can turn into when we surround ourselves with the wrong voices. The Acts community gives us a model we should shoot for when we are looking for people to walk with in our faith. For good or for bad, your community will shape your faith trajectory. Choose people who have the faith you want, because you will end up growing a faith that looks like theirs.

REFLECTION QUESTIONS

1. As you compare the communities of Numbers 13 and Acts 2, which is most similar to your community? Do you surround yourself with voices of doubt or voices of faith? Does your community strengthen or weaken you?

2. Looking at Matthew 27 and 2 Samuel 12, how do Pilate and David differ when it comes to hearing the truth? Has anyone ever told you truth that was hard to hear? Do you tend to respond defensively or humbly to people who tell you difficult truth?

3. Looking at the communities in Exodus 17 and Acts 4, are you more likely to respond to uncertain

circumstances with courage because of your memories of faith or fear for the unknown? What changes (if any) do you need to make about the community you surround yourself with?

10

Your Faith Is Part of a Bigger Story

WHAT YOU *DON'T* KNOW is the space where God is working. What you *do* know is the space where you live. Living by faith is knowing that what is in front of you right now is part of a story that you can't see.

I lived this truth when I got that phone call in my Orange County apartment asking if I was interested in interviewing for a job at a church in Santa Barbara. The call led to a move, which three years later led to a marriage, which for two reasons changed my life. On my wedding day, I became a wife and a stepmom, and a year later, my stepson's biological mom moved to Australia. Becoming a stepmom was never the kind of motherhood I dreamed about growing up, but being the full-time stepmom of a six-year-old boy graced and altered both of our lives. When my stepson turned seventeen, I wrote a book called *Grace-Filled Stepparenting* and asked him to lend his voice to the last chapter. Our book has been able to encourage hundreds of stepparents who I never would have been connected to if I hadn't met my husband and stepped into this role.

> Living by faith is knowing that what is in front of you right now is part of a story that you can't see.

Two years ago, my stepson made the decision to get baptized, and my husband and I stood by him in the ocean with our church community, watching. He recently became a volunteer leader for the junior high youth group and told us that God has been speaking to him about a possible ministry call. He is now on the worship team at our church and has continued to stay strongly connected to the community that helped raise him.

All of this unfolded because I took a job at a church in Santa Barbara because I had just broken an engagement and was able to say yes to that call.

How strange it is to retrace our steps.

In that apartment where my life had fallen apart, God picked up the pieces and carried me into an unimaginable future. My husband, our church community, my stepson, his baptism, my book, dozens of stepparents, and my stepson's potential calling to ministry are the results of a decision to pick myself up and step through the door in front of me, into a story I couldn't see.

The decisions you make in the time and space you live will be part of God's unseen and unimaginable story. If you lean into your situation and stay open, God may have you on the cusp of something wonderful to come. Dark seasons often position us in front of a story that we can't see—and that story may invite you to play a part you can't imagine.

You have to trust where you are right now for what might be ahead.

Difficult seasons can be the most important chapters in our faith story. What you decide to do when you are in them makes a difference in what happens next. The willingness to trust God's ways and timing impacts your role in the story to come—and that will not only include people around you but ahead of you. But in order to keep believing what you can't see, you need hope from other faith stories to persevere through the hard parts of your own. That's the reason I wrote this book.

There is a chapter in the book of Hebrews where we can find the condensed collection of many Old Testament faith stories. Hebrews 11 is called "the hall of fame of faith" because it reads like an awards ceremony for people who bravely lived their faith in the unknown. Some people in the chapter saw parts of their stories resolved, others did not, but they all made decisions of faith that were part of a longer timeline. Hebrews 11 gives a snapshot of how their stories fit together in the eternal story—which is the stage where all our faith stories are lived.

History reveals that you and I arrived in the middle of an ongoing story. We realize this truth as we grow up and learn what happened before us, and how things will keep going after we leave. The way you live your life is largely determined by whether you believe this life is all there is or that your life is part of God's eternal story. Your belief about life and God will impact how you live the time you are here.

If you believe your life is part of a story you can't fully see, you will have a different perspective on interrupted plans and unwanted circumstances. Instead of always fighting your way out of these circumstances, you will look to find the purpose of where you are. You will live—and die—differently because you know your life has a purpose beyond your understanding. Hebrews 11 was written to celebrate people who lived from that perspective, and they are commended—not for what they accomplished but for the way their faith was lived.

HEBREWS 11:1–11: The Timeline Is Longer Than Life

Hebrews 11:1 says that faith is "confidence in what we hope for and assurance about what we do not see," calling us to live under an invisible reality. To have any success at it, this invisible reality has to be reestablished daily, if not hourly, because what we *do* see often contradicts our belief. Creation is one way to remind ourselves of this unseen reality because "the universe was formed at God's command, so that what is seen was not made out of what was visible" (v. 3). Looking at what "just happens" in nature and the world around us points to either an undirected, miraculous orchestration of atoms and molecules, or to God. The story behind the story peeks through when we breathe, feel, watch the sun rise, or see a baby born, and experience the complexity of all that is orchestrated to make those things possible. The universe draws us to acknowledge there must be an invisible reality of something more than we can see.

The writer of Hebrews celebrates people's faith with the backdrop of God's bigger story. Hebrews 11 gives us a summary of those who stepped out in faith during the time in which they lived and even includes some things that happened after they died. For example, in verse 4, when the writer speaks of Abel's brief earthly life and his sacrifice, he adds that Abel "still speaks, even though he is dead"—pointing us to the eternal timeline of Abel's story. With this curious phrase, he indicates that the meaning of our life does not end when we die.

The theme of Hebrews 11 is that our life has meaning that we only partially see. Some of the decisions we make by faith will impact people and situations to come. The writer of Hebrews has a pattern of commending people for their acts of faith and then points to the unseen reality behind their earthly story. Our stories of faith find their true meaning on a longer timeline than the length of our lives.

Hebrews 11:6 emphasizes what the rest of the Bible points to: "Without faith it is impossible to please God, because anyone who comes to him must believe that he exists and that he rewards those who earnestly seek him." This verse reaffirms what we already know: we can't have a relationship with an invisible God without believing God exists. And because faith grows by believing things that are unseen, the rest of the chapter celebrates those who stood in front of the unseen and who responded in faith.

Hebrews 11 shows how decisions of faith are part of a longer story by beginning with Abraham's journey. Abraham never saw all that would unfold when he was told to leave his home. Verse 8 says, "Abraham, when called to go to a place he would later receive as his inheritance, obeyed and went, even though he did not know where he was going." He said yes to the decision God put before him, and that "yes" impacted many people to come. Abraham had to live in tents—as did his son Isaac and grandson Jacob—because they were heirs to a promise that would unfold after their lifetime. Abraham said yes to beginning a story that would outlast his life.

Abraham would never settle in or build on the land that he was told to claim; it would end up being the home of his descendants. Included in Abraham's step of faith was believing there would actually *be* descendants, since Sarah was barren and he had no children at the time.

Abraham's journey of faith speaks to ours when we don't understand what God is doing. He had to say yes to promises that would unfold as he stepped out in faith. Hebrews 11:11 alludes to the chapter in Abraham's story we already know—that

Abraham's promised child didn't come until he was one hundred years old and Sarah was ninety. So Abraham moved to a land for descendants who would come after him, before there was any prospect of Sarah bearing a child. Hebrews 11:12 proclaims what eventually ensued: "And so from this one man, and he as good as dead, came descendants as numerous as the stars in the sky and as countless as the sand on the seashore." When Abraham left, this was the future he had to trust God to achieve.

Abraham's story included three gigantic steps of faith: heading to an unknown land, believing in an unseen child, and (we'll soon see) surviving a terrifying proposition. Though his faith hit some bumps over his lifetime, Abraham persevered—and he lived all three decisions of faith as a model for how to live ours. Hebrews 11 makes it clear that Abraham, along with everyone else in this chapter, was called to live a story of faith on a bigger, eternal timeline. They responded to decisions they could see, while God wove their faith into a bigger story that would outlive their earthly lives.

HEBREWS 11:13–22: Resolution Is Seen from a Distance

Abraham is mentioned three times in Hebrews 11 because he lived three dramatic (and increasingly emotional) faith stories. Because of his age when Isaac was born, Abraham didn't get to see his grandchildren or great-grandchildren, let alone the tribes of Israel that would come from his grandson's sons. Verse 13 describes what it meant for Abraham and others to live by faith, and it is worth thinking about when it comes to our own lives: "All these people were still living by faith when they died. They did not receive the things promised; they only saw them and welcomed them from a distance."

According to this verse, we may take some of what is unseen to our deathbed. Because we live our faith story on an eternal timeline, we won't get to see things completely resolved. Even the glimpses we *do* get are just the beginning, because when prayers are answered, we have no idea of all that God is going to do with them. Hebrews 11 gives us a peek at the view we will get in eternity when we see how God weaves together stories from our earthly lives.

Thinking back to my decision to move to Santa Barbara, I realize that even with the story I now know, there is still much about the story that I don't know. My stepson will grow up, may marry and have children, and may continue to do ministry, and his faith will touch people in ways I'll never see. The stepparents who read the words my stepson and I wrote in our book may take something of value into their stepparenting, which may impact future families and children. The story of my broken engagement and later-in-life marriage may be passed on to encourage people I don't know, or be used after I'm gone to bring someone hope. Your story is being formed not just for you and the people in your life right now, but for lives that will come after you. You will not receive all the promises that come from your acts of faith, because as verse 13 says, you will still be living by faith when you die. Your faith story is bigger than you, and it will last longer than your life.

> Your story is being formed not just for you and the people in your life right now, but for lives that will come after you.

It's this knowledge of a God who works even after our death that led Abraham to his third act of faith, when he was presented with the unthinkable. The son who finally had come when it was biologically impossible was to be offered as a sacrifice to prove Abraham's trust in God (v. 17). So many times I've read this story and been disturbed, until a pastor I greatly admired gave me some historical context for what God might have been doing in this difficult text.

In Abraham's culture, many people believed in gods who demanded child sacrifice. It's possible that in this test of Abraham's faith, God wanted to rectify that demand in Abraham's belief. By taking Abraham through the process of thinking this kind of sacrifice would be demanded of him, God was asking Abraham to trust that He would provide a substitutionary sacrifice. This understanding is indicated in Genesis 22:8, when Isaac asks Abraham where the sacrifice is, and Abraham tells Isaac that "God himself will provide the lamb."

Abraham's words to Isaac are his ultimate act of trust, and Hebrews 11:17–19 illustrates that by this time, Abraham's faith has grown to confidence. By trusting God with the precious son who had been promised to him, Abraham demonstrated his confidence that he knew God would somehow hold them both. Confidence is God's goal for us, and knowing that our lives—as well as the people we love—exist on an eternal timeline helps us hold on to our faith even in death.

The next three stories in Hebrews 11 illustrate what life looks like when we are welcoming things that have been promised from a distance. When our life on earth is ending, we can have confidence that the story we took part in will go on. That's what Isaac knew when, at the end of his life, he blessed Jacob and Esau with regard to their future. The blessing didn't unfold as Isaac thought it would because Jacob had deceived him, but Isaac gave both sons blessings—and trusted God's bigger plan. Later in his life, Esau came to trust God's plan too—even though the way it unfolded wasn't what he expected or wanted. Isaac's blessing to both his sons set them up for the story of grace between them that would unfold after his death.

Jacob went even further into the future than his father; when he blessed Joseph's sons, he was reaching beyond his sons to his grandchildren. Hebrews 11:21 adds that as he blessed them, he "worshiped as he leaned on the top of his staff." It's curious that the writer of Hebrews would include this detail, until we look into the future and see that Joseph's sons became the tribes of Israel, and eventually birthed the generation of Israelites who were led out of Egypt. When Jacob worshiped by leaning on the top of his staff, it may have been a foreshadowing of the staff used by Moses to free his descendants—a story only seen from a distance because it was still ahead.

Hebrews 11 tells us that Joseph, too, spoke into the future, following the footsteps of his father, Jacob, and his grandfather, Isaac. Verse 22 says that at the end of his life, Joseph "spoke about the exodus of the Israelites from Egypt and gave instructions concerning the burial of his bones." Joseph didn't end his life just by blessing children or grandchildren but by giving instructions for his great-great-grandchildren, who would be alive when the exodus happened. When you look back to Exodus 13:19, you can see that Joseph's instructions were passed down through four generations, because Joseph's bones were with Moses when the Israelites escaped.

We see in these stories what is true about all our lives—we are part of a story that started before us and will outlive us. Joseph's instructions about carrying his bones out of Egypt were meant for people in the future who he didn't even know or see. Hebrews 11 celebrates people for living their lives with an understanding of this eternal timeline—they lived by faith for what would unfold in the future. Any resolution they saw they only welcomed at a distance, but they ended their lives living their part.

Verse 13 also calls the people in this chapter "foreigners and strangers on earth," meaning that they understood their origins were from somewhere different. The writer of Hebrews says they knew they were citizens of another country—a heavenly one—and this "better country" is where they were longing to go when they died (vv. 15–16). This is another indication that our time on earth is part of something bigger—we arrive and leave in the middle of a longer story. It's also clear from the imagery of a "heavenly country" in these verses that earth is not our final home.

The stories at the end of this chapter reinforce that truth.

HEBREWS 11:32–12:1: Our Stories Are Connected

Generally in an awards ceremony, the biggest awards are given at the end so the ceremony can build to a crescendo. With that in mind, it may seem odd that Hebrews 11 ends with people who were persecuted, tortured, imprisoned, and mistreated, carrying unrealized faith promises into their deaths. What we might view as stories of failure, Hebrews 11 holds up as the highest awards of faith.

It is further evidence of what Jesus's death and resurrection taught us—what looks like the end is *not* the end; it's the middle of the story. If your life is positioned on an eternal timeline, death is *not* the end of you. What you see happen *during* your life is not all that happens *because* of your life. Your story of faith might just have its greatest impact after you are dead. Certainly that was true of Jesus.

Hebrews 11 ends with people who bravely lived out stories of apparent defeat—and proclaims them victorious. After listing all the stories of faith that experienced miraculous intervention (vv. 29–34), the writer of Hebrews ends the chapter with a much gloomier report:

> There were others who were tortured, refusing to be released so that they might gain an even better resurrection. Some faced jeers and flogging, and even chains and imprisonment.

They were put to death by stoning; they were sawed in two; they were killed by the sword. They went about in sheepskins and goatskins, destitute, persecuted and mistreated—the world was not worthy of them. They wandered in deserts and mountains, living in caves and in holes in the ground.

Hebrews 11:35–38

Not exactly children's bedtime reading—more like an epic war story. And yet, this paragraph of people who courageously faced their death is the climax of the hall of fame of faith. We can only conclude that faith is meant for more than this life.

So often we believe that faith is rewarded by getting the things we hope for, and we assume those things will happen within our lifetime. But this chapter assumes something else—the thing we hope for most comes after our death. Hebrews 11 is a chapter to avoid if your faith is measured by health, ease, pain avoidance, and material blessing. This chapter emphasizes that resurrection is the hope our faith ultimately lives for, because no matter how much we avoid this truth, we (and everyone we love) will face the end of life. According to Hebrews 11, the confidence you have in the face of death may be your greatest act of faith.

I am reminded of my cousin Gary, who served for thirty years as a firefighter. He and his wife, Debbie, had two children, and the child who had some special needs brought the family to a deeper faith. After Gary retired, he and Debbie were in a season of well-deserved blessing until his throat developed some sores that started concerning them. His years of fire service left a residue that turned out to be cancer, but even with this unwelcome diagnosis, Gary determined he would win the fight. Through chemo and radiation, burning sores, and sleepless nights, finally, barely being able to breathe, he did.

After a glorious two-and-a-half years of living cancer free, an oncology report suddenly revealed the dreaded cancer had returned and somehow spread to Gary's liver. He was given just enough hope to enter into the agonizing battle a second time. So he did. Months of chemotherapy treatments later, when the doctor told him the cancer had not only spread but that he had a matter of days to live, Gary gave up the battle. That's when his faith became unleashed.

Gary began consoling those who came to console him that he was the lucky one because of the future that awaited him. He no longer feared the news that his cancer would beat him; he beat his cancer through hope in the face of death. The joy that emanated from a man reduced to skin and bones was otherworldly, and it drew a strange envy from those who witnessed it. Gary lived Hebrews 11 faith up to the door of his death. It's even clear that faith carried him past that door because of the miraculous things Debbie witnessed after he died.

The end of Gary's life is the goal of our faith: to hold on until we see the life that waits for us. Up until the moment we die, we only know life after death exists through faith. In 1 Corinthians 13:12, Paul describes our pre-eternal vision by saying, "Now we see only a reflection as in a mirror." Another translation says, "Now we see things imperfectly, like puzzling reflections in a mirror" (NLT), which aptly describes the way things look. Paul goes on to say, "Now I know in part; then I shall know fully, even as I am fully known," implying that after death, we will finally see what God sees. Until that moment, we will only see far away glimpses and flawed reflections of the spiritual realities we will someday see. Because we live in front of eternity, the writer of Hebrews showcases people who lived, made hard decisions, and died, banking on their belief.

The culminating verses of Hebrews 11 reveal the enormous canvas of our faith story. These last two verses are especially helpful when we don't see things resolved in the way or in the timing that we asked. The writer of Hebrews links us with the people who lived before us, joining us together in God's bigger story. He indicates that together our stories will make sense of the unresolved pieces that they (or we) weren't able to see:

> These were all commended for their faith, yet none of them received what had been promised, since God had planned something better for us so that only together with us would they be made perfect.
>
> Hebrews 11:39–40

How do we understand these verses except to conclude that all our faith stories are connected? The way we live our story of faith is part of something that doesn't end with our death. The writer of Hebrews says God's plan for something better is unfolding—whether we see things resolved or not, experience miraculous healing or not, live many years or not—because our faith stories are part of a bigger unseen story. Only when we cross over into eternity will we see the complete part we played.

Until then, we find inspiration in people who live faith courageously in front of us. We find encouragement in the way difficult circumstances brought us to people who are now indispensable to us, and who, without those circumstances, we never would have met. The hand of God is traced in retrospect because we live in the mystery of not fully seeing what is happening. As I dreamed in this chapter of what might become of my stepson, his future, and people I might touch that I'll never know, you, too, can know there will be a future which will unfold in ways that you can't see. The phrase "only together with us would they be made perfect" (v. 40) aptly describes the way God moves in our stories. As we've seen in the previous chapters of this book, God's bigger purpose connects us through all the joys and sorrows and uncertainties of our lives.

The last verse of Hebrews 11 seems to silently allude to the coming of Jesus, who came to earth after the lives celebrated in this chapter. The story of Jesus's birth, death, and resurrection is the story *we* know that they didn't; Jesus made possible the "something better for us" that God had planned. But we are all still awaiting the future that Jesus promised would come—when He will return, and evil and suffering and death will no longer have power. Until then, we live by faith in the story we have, in the greater story we know—through our belief.

So what is the concluding hope Hebrews 11 gives us for bravely living out our stories? You may be surprised, because the concluding hope is actually found in Hebrews 12. The end of Hebrews 11 is not actually the end, which is evident in Hebrews 12:1 with the word *"Therefore."* The Bibles we have now are partitioned in chapters and verses, but the original Scriptures were unpunctuated documents, so this chapter bled into the next. Hebrews 12:1 is the resounding wake-up call that ends the Hebrews 11 hall of fame of faith:

> Therefore, since we are surrounded by such a great cloud of witnesses, let us throw off everything that hinders and the sin that so easily entangles. And let us run with perseverance the race marked out for us.

Here's a tip about studying the Bible: the *next* verse—even when it's found in the next chapter—clarifies and expands the previous verse. This verse in Hebrews 12 gives us the exclamation point of Hebrews 11. These stories were documented to inspire us to lean in and live our own. The resounding call to "run with perseverance the race marked out for us" (Hebrews

12:1) both encourages and urges us to live our story. With the stories of Hebrews 11 and people like Gary who have gone before us, we become emboldened to live our call.

Life is the gift God has given us. The way we live is our gift back to God. Our time here, whether minimal or full of years, pales in comparison to God's eternal timeline. The Bible makes it clear that we will be remembered by the life we live while we are here. And somewhere in the unseen, we have a cloud of witnesses cheering us on.

REFLECTION QUESTIONS

1. What verses in Hebrews 11:1–10 show that your life here is not where your life ends? Does knowing your life on earth is only a small part of an eternal timeline make you want to live differently or just keep going the way you are? What (if any) changes do you want to make?

2. Hebrews 11:13 indicates that resolution is not always complete when we leave this earth, and some things will only be resolved in eternity. Does this make you feel encouraged or discouraged? Why? What would you like to see resolved?

3. Hebrews 11:40 gives us a huge spiritual insight about the way our stories fit together. Have you seen any hint of this in your life and relationships already? How does this change your perspective—knowing your choices and actions may have more meaning than you think?

Acknowledgments

Special thanks to

Jeff Braun, who believed in this book before it was started

Elisa Haugen, who encouraged me by saying God spoke to her through an early draft

The readers of *40 Verses to Ignite Your Faith,* for without them, this book would not have been written

Melissa Johnston, who prayed me through the struggle of expressing important thoughts

And Jere and Jordan, who ate very few home-cooked dinners and worked around me as I wrote for nine months in our little home

Laurie Polich Short is a popular speaker, author, and part of the teaching team at Ocean Hills Covenant Church in Santa Barbara, California. A graduate of Fuller Theological Seminary, Laurie has spoken to more than 500,000 people at conferences, colleges, churches, and denominational events around the country, and she has been featured on PBS, *Focus on the Family*, *World* magazine, and more. Find out more at laurieshort.com.

More from Laurie Polich Short

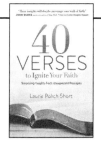

In this powerful book, author and speaker Laurie Polich Short mines Scripture, revealing insights and promises from 40 verses we often overlook. Digging in to these in-between verses, she unearths fresh wisdom, guidance, and encouragement that will help you seek and experience God in new, dynamic ways.

40 Verses to Ignite Your Faith

BETHANYHOUSE

 Stay up to date on your favorite books and authors with our free e-newsletters. Sign up today at bethanyhouse.com.

 facebook.com/BHPnonfiction

 @bethany_house

 @bethany_house_nonfiction